KOUZES
POSNER

D1712789

THE LEADERSHIP CHALLENGE VALUES CARDS

FACILITATOR'S GUIDE

JAMES M. KOUZES AND BARRY Z. POSNER
WITH JO BELL AND RENEE HARNESS

Package ISBN: 978-0-470-57895-7

Acquiring Editor: Marisa Kelley
Development Editor: Leslie Stephen
Editor: Rebecca Taff
Composition: MPS
Printed in the United States of America

Director of Development: Kathleen Dolan Davies
Production Editor: Dawn Kilgore
Manufacturing Supervisor: Becky Morgan
Design: Riezeboz Holzbaur Group

Printing 10 9 8 7 6 5 4 3 2 1

CONTENTS

Contents

WEBSITE TABLE OF CONTENTS

Our readers are invited to download customizable materials from this book. The following materials are available FREE with the purchase of this book at: www.leadershipchallenge.com/go/tlcvaluescards

    The following username and password are required for accessing these materials:

Username: leader
Password: value

ABOUT THE AUTHORS

Jim Kouzes** and **Barry Posner** are coauthors of the award-winning and best-selling book, *The Leadership Challenge*. This book was selected as one of the top 10 books on leadership of all time (according to *The 100 Best Business Books of All Time*), won the James A. Hamilton Hospital Administrators' Book-of-the-Year Award and the Critics' Choice Award from the nation's book review editors, was a *BusinessWeek* best-seller, and has sold over 1.8 million copies in more than twenty languages. Jim and Barry have coauthored more than a dozen other leadership books, including *A Leader's Legacy*—selected by *Soundview Executive Book Summaries* as one of the top thirty books of the year—*Credibility: How Leaders Gain It and Lose It, Why People Demand It*—chosen by *Industry Week* as one of its year's five best management books—*Encouraging the Heart, The Student Leadership Challenge,* and *The Academic Administrator's Guide to Exemplary Leadership.* They also developed the highly acclaimed *Leadership Practices Inventory* (LPI), a 360-degree questionnaire for assessing leadership behavior, which is one of the most widely used leadership assessment instruments in the world. More than 400 doctoral dissertations and academic research projects have been based on the Five Practices of Exemplary Leadership model.

Among the honors and awards that Jim and Barry have received are the American Society for Training and Development's (ASTD) highest award for their Distinguished Contribution to Workplace Learning and Performance; Management/Leadership Educators of the Year by the International Management Council (this honor puts them in the company of Ken Blanchard, Stephen Covey, Peter Drucker, Edward Deming, Frances Hesselbein, Lee Iacocca,

Rosabeth Moss Kanter, Norman Vincent Peale, and Tom Peters, who are all past recipients of the award); and named among the Top 50 Leadership Coaches in the nation (according to *Coaching for Leadership*).

Jim and Barry are frequent conference speakers, and each has conducted leadership development programs for hundreds of organizations, including Apple, Applied Materials, ARCO, AT&T, Australia Post, Bank of America, Bose, Charles Schwab, Cisco Systems, Community Leadership Association, Conference Board of Canada, Consumers Energy, Dell Computer, Deloitte Touche, Dorothy Wylie Nursing Leadership Institute, Egon Zehnder International, Federal Express, Gymboree, Hewlett-Packard, IBM, Jobs DR-Singapore, Johnson & Johnson, Kaiser Foundation Health Plans and Hospitals, L. L. Bean, Lawrence Livermore National Labs, Lucile Packard Children's Hospital, Merck, Mervyn's, Motorola, NetApp, Northrop Grumman, Roche Bioscience, Siemens, Standard Aero, Sun Microsystems, 3M, Toyota, the U.S. Postal Service, United Way, USAA, Verizon, VISA, and The Walt Disney Company.

Jo Bell and Renee Harness are managing partners at Third Eye Leadership, whose mission is to inspire organizational strength with courage and vision. They are experts in strengthening the organizational bottom line through evidence-based leadership experiences, such as The Leadership Challenge Model. They are contributors to the second, third, and fourth editions of *The Leadership Challenge*, master facilitators of The Leadership Challenge® Workshop, and executive coaches utilizing the *Leadership Practices Inventory*.

Jo Bell. The seed of Jo's passion for leadership sprouted in a serendipitous introduction to Jim Kouzes in 1987 at a medical symposium; shortly afterward Jo began her leadership mentorship with him. Jo has been a master facilitator since 1998. Jo's earlier career in healthcare, which spanned seventeen years as a hematologist and director of clinical laboratories, gave Jo a strong foundation as a leader and a manager in understanding human behavior, motivations, and the impact on the core business. Jo is known for developing lasting customer partnerships through her genuine passion for leadership and her astute attention to the strategic alignment of the leadership development implementation. Jo has a bachelor's degree in clinical laboratory medicine, a master's degree in organization development, and a doctorate in hematology.

A Personal Message from Jo: *"I envision myself as an architect in designing an environment that stewards learning and leadership—one that refreshes and challenges. I consider myself a "Scout 4 What If!"… a life-long learner with a robust inquisitive nature. I believe the greatness for leadership lies within every individual—sometimes fossilized from insecurity, unawareness, or the belief that it's reserved for only a few great men, a few great women, or the higher levels within an organization. It is my personal commitment to encourage others to stretch—to learn—to breathe life into—to seize the opportunity to lead. It is my charter to help others embrace leadership as an identifiable set of skills and practices available to all of us."*

Renee Harness. Renee has a discerning eye for creating a climate that appeals to the needs of leaders as learners and becomes a catalyst for open minds. Renee has been a facilitator of The Leadership Challenge since 1999, and a Master Facilitator since 2006. She has led organization development, training, and effectiveness initiatives in corporations and academia for more than sixteen years. Her roles in companies such as Charles Schwab & Co., Inc., and Roche Diagnostics, as well as several Indiana state universities, have focused on engaging the leader within people at all levels to create a climate of leadership and results through people. Her experience includes large-scale implementation of leadership programs at the executive, first-line manager, and employee levels. Renee holds a master of science degree in sociology.

A Personal Message from Renee: *"Leadership is not only a science, it is an art. And just as in fine art, there is more below the surface of our leadership than meets the eye. What sparks my passion about* The Leadership Challenge *is that I am not only helping leaders find the art of their own leadership, but that this has a positive impact on the lives of the people around these leaders. My commitment is to help leaders fully engage, develop, and excite the people they work with, creating an environment in which leaders get results through the passionate involvement of their people."*

INTRODUCTION

"The instrument of leadership is the self, and mastery of the art of leadership comes from the mastery of the self."
—Jim Kouzes and Barry Posner

Throughout their international best-selling book, *The Leadership Challenge*, Jim Kouzes and Barry Posner tell stories of ordinary people who have mobilized others to get extraordinary things done in virtually every arena of organized activity. They talk about men and women, young and old, from a variety of organizations—small and large, public and private, manufacturing and services, high-tech and low-tech. These leaders are not famous people or mega-stars. They're people who might live next door or work in the next cubicle. Kouzes and Posner focus on leaders like this because they firmly believe that leadership is not about position, but about relationships, credibility, and what people *do*.

"Ordinary" individuals can mobilize others to get extraordinary things done in organizations by practicing The Five Practices of Exemplary Leadership®, the leadership model Kouzes and Posner developed from a research project begun more than twenty-five years ago. To answer the question, "What is it that people actually *do* to get extraordinary things done in organizations?" Kouzes and Posner collected thousands of stories in which people described what they did when they were at their "personal best" in leading others. The personal bests were experiences in which their study respondents, in their own estimation, set their individual leadership standards of excellence.

THE FIVE PRACTICES OF EXEMPLARY LEADERSHIP®

From their analysis of thousands of personal-best leadership experiences, Kouzes and Posner found that, despite differences in people's individual stories, all the experiences followed remarkably similar patterns of action in a wide range of settings. As they looked deeper into the dynamic process of leadership, through case analyses and survey questionnaires, they uncovered five practices common to the respondents' personal-best leadership experiences.

When getting extraordinary things done in organizations, leaders engage in these Five Practices of Exemplary Leadership®:

- Model the Way
- Inspire a Shared Vision
- Challenge the Process
- Enable Others to Act
- Encourage the Heart

Over time and across continents, these five practices have endured as a model for how leaders mobilize others to transform values into actions, visions into realities, obstacles into innovations, separateness into solidarity, and risks into rewards. Even though the context might have changed since Kouzes and Posner began their research, the conclusion has remained the same: leadership is a set of skills and abilities that can be learned by almost anyone who has the desire and commitment to improve.

Embedded in The Five Practices of Exemplary Leadership® are behaviors that serve as the basis for learning to lead. Kouzes and Posner call these The Ten Commitments of Leadership (see Table 1).

TABLE 1. The Five Practices and Ten Commitments of Exemplary Leadership

Model the Way

1. Clarify values by finding your voice and affirming shared ideals.

2. Set the example by aligning actions and shared values.

Inspire a Shared Vision

3. Envision the future by imagining exciting and ennobling possibilities.

4. Enlist others in a common vision by appealing to shared aspirations.

Challenge the Process

5. Search for opportunities by seizing the initiative and by looking outward for innovative ways to improve.

6. Experiment and take risks by constantly generating small wins and learning from experience.

Enable Others to Act

7. Foster collaboration by building trust and facilitating relationships.

8. Strengthen others by increasing self-determination and developing competence.

Encourage the Heart

9. Recognize contributions by showing appreciation for individual excellence.

10. Celebrate the values and victories by creating a spirit of community.

The *Leadership Practices Inventory* further translates The Five Practices into behavioral statements so that people can assess their skills and use this feedback to improve their leadership abilities.

The research data from hundreds of thousands of people consistently show that leaders who more frequently engage in The Five Practices are more likely to be identified as effective leaders. That's a key outcome for all the learning activities built on *The Leadership Challenge*: For leaders to learn what The Five Practices of Exemplary Leadership® entail and develop their ability to comfortably engage in them more frequently than they are doing today. The activities in this guide focus on Model the Way and are specifically designed to help leaders first to clarify their own values, then to identify shared values of their teams, and finally to learn ways to align their actions with those values.

MODEL THE WAY: CLARIFY VALUES, SET THE EXAMPLE*

A significant finding of Kouzes and Posner's research is that credibility is the foundation of leadership.* To be able to take strong stands, challenge the status quo, and point constituents in new directions, leaders must be highly credible. Constituents must believe in their leaders who ask them to go to an uncertain future. As Kouzes and Posner state in their "First Law of Leadership": *If you don't believe in the messenger, you won't believe the message.* So how do leaders establish credibility? When people decide whether a leader is credible, or believable, they first listen to the words and then watch the actions. If leaders walk the talk, if they practice what they preach, people are more willing to entrust them with their livelihood and even their lives. Thus, exemplary leaders know and follow "The Kouzes-Posner Second Law of Leadership": *DWYSYWD: Do What You Say You Will Do.*

This section adapted, with permission, from James M. Kouzes and Barry Z. Posner, The Leadership Challenge (4th ed.). San Francisco: Jossey-Bass, 2007, pp. 38–41, 47–67.

Model the Way leads directly from the "say" and "do" dimensions of the DWYSYWD definition of credibility. The two Commitments (behaviors) embedded in this practice are (1) the clarification of a set of values and (2) being an example of those values to others. This consistent living out of values demonstrates honesty and trustworthiness. People trust leaders when their deeds and words match.

To walk the talk, you have to have a talk to walk. To do what you say, you have to know what you want to say. To earn and sustain personal credibility, you must first be able to clearly articulate deeply held beliefs. In other words, you can't be the messenger until you're clear about what you believe. To become a credible leader you have to fully comprehend the values, beliefs, principles, standards, ethics, and ideals that drive you. Then you have to communicate your beliefs in your own voice, in ways that are true to the unique person you are.

Being clear about one's values makes a significant difference in behavior at work, Kouzes and Posner's research has found. For example, they have learned that it is personal values clarity that drives commitment to organizations, as shown in Figure 1, where the number in each of the four cells represents the average level of commitment people have to their organizations as it relates to the degree of their clarity about personal and organizational values. The people who have the greatest clarity about both personal and organizational values have the highest degree of commitment to the organization.

But leaders aren't just speaking for themselves when they talk about the values that should guide decisions and actions. They must also be sure there's agreement on a set of shared values among all people they lead. Leaders who stand for values that do not represent the team's or organization's ideals won't be able to mobilize people to act as one. Exemplary leaders must be able to gain consensus on a common cause and a common set of principles. They must be able to affirm shared ideals and build a community of shared values.

When there's congruence between individual values and organizational values, Kouzes and Posner have shown, there's significant payoff for leaders and their organizations. Shared values make a

FIGURE 1. The Impact of Values Clarity on Commitment

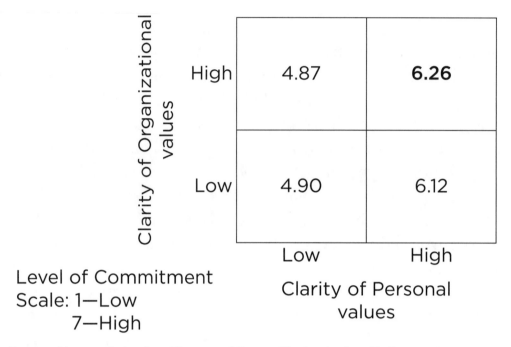

Level of Commitment
Scale: 1—Low
       7—High

significant and positive difference in work attitudes and performance; they are the foundation for building productive and genuine working relationships.

THE LEADERSHIP CHALLENGE VALUES CARDS

The Leadership Challenge (TLC) Values Cards and activities were created to provide leaders with the opportunity to deepen knowledge and alignment around personal and team values. Kouzes and Posner's research has shown that leadership is an identifiable set of skills and abilities that can be learned by almost anyone who has the desire and commitment to improve. Long used in The Leadership Challenge® Workshop, the The Leadership Challenge Values Card deck can be used with leaders who have just been introduced to *The Leadership Challenge* as well as those who have been through the workshop or other TLC-derived learning experiences.

The deck contains fifty-two cards with words representing personal or team values printed on them. For example, the first card is Achievement/Success, Creativity, Teamwork (see Table 2). There are also four blank cards so participants can add any value(s) they hold that are not represented in the deck.

TABLE 2. The Leadership Challenge Values Cards

Achievement/Success	Autonomy
Beauty	Challenge
Communication	Competence
Competition	Courage
Creativity	Curiosity
Decisiveness	Dependability
Discipline	Diversity
Effectiveness	Empathy
Equality	Family
Flexibility	Friendship
Freedom	Growth
Happiness	Harmony
Health	Honesty/Integrity
Hope	Humor
Independence	Innovation
Intelligence	Love/Affection
Loyalty	Open-Mindedness
Patience	Power
Productivity	Prosperity/Wealth

(Continued)

TABLE 2. The Leadership Challenge Values Cards (*Continued*)

Quality	Recognition
Respect	Risk Taking
Security	Service
Simplicity	Spirituality/Faith
Strength	Teamwork
Trust	Truth
Variety	Wisdom
_____	_____
_____	_____

The activities in this Guide represent just a few ways the The Leadership Challenge Values Cards might be used to help leaders practice effective leadership skills. We encourage leaders and facilitators to come up with other ways to use the cards to improve their leadership practices.

HOW TO USE THIS FACILITATOR'S GUIDE

Overall Flow of Activities

There are three types of The Leadership Challenge Values Cards learning activities in this Guide:

- *Introductory Activities*—to introduce the concepts associated with the cards
- *Personal Values Drive Commitment Activities*—to help leaders gain greater clarity on personal values and how to align their actions with them

- *Shared Values Make the Difference Activities*—to help leaders affirm shared ideals and align ongoing actions

These activities are presented in the recommended order of delivery, and each activity has any prerequisite activities noted. The sequence of activities is

Introductory Activities

Activity 1	Values Matter Board Game
Activity 2	Leaders Tell Us . . .

Personal Values Drive Commitment Activities

Activity 3	Values Card Sort
Activity 4	Aligning Actions with Values
Activity 5	Are My Actions Aligned?
Activity 6	Values and Individual Interactions: How Values Influence Our Interactions
Activity 7	Case Studies: Values as Coaching Tool
Activity 8	Your Challenging Situation: Values as Coaching Tool

Shared Values Make the Difference Activities

Activity 9	Shared Team Values: Keeping Personal Values in Mind
Activity 10	Creating Team Values
Activity 11	Organizational, Team, and Personal Values in Action

Activity Design and Description

The design and description for the The Leadership Challenge Values Card activities includes:

- *Activity Overview*—A brief description of the activity
- *Purpose*—The purpose, objective(s), or outcome(s)
- *Participants*—Minimum, maximum, and best group size

- *Prerequisites*—Prerequisite The Leadership Challenge Values Card activities and recommended pre-work, if any
- *Time*—Recommended time for conducting the activity
- *Supplies and Resources*—Materials required
- *Facilitator Notes*—Sequence of events and instructions to the facilitator, including an overview, activity setup, introducing the activity, guidance for participants, debriefing and trigger questions, and the like
- *Variations*—Alternative ways to set up or conduct the activities
- *Coach's Notes*—Where appropriate, contains ideas for coaches who are working with individual leaders on how to adapt the activities to one-on-one interactions.

Suggestions for Successful Results

Planning and Preparing

This Facilitator's Guide walks you through the process of planning and delivering the The Leadership Challenge Values Card activities. It includes step-by-step instructions, and in some cases a "script" for setting up, conducting, and debriefing the activities. You can use the script as is or adapt it to meet the needs of your group.

Here are some suggestions for planning and preparing for successful results:

- Read this Facilitator's Guide carefully. The more familiar you are with the material, the easier it will be to facilitate its use with others.
- Think of stories and examples from your organization that you could use to further illustrate each of The Five Practices. This is particularly helpful in case study activities with the The Leadership Challenge Values Cards.
- Become more familiar with The Five Practices of Exemplary Leadership® model by reading *The Leadership Challenge,* which

includes many stories to illustrate The Five Practices. Also visit www.leadershipchallenge.com for a wealth of information on the model, validity and reliability data, related materials, FAQs, facilitation tips and techniques, and more.

- Determine whether to make any changes to the activity design. For example, you may prefer to adjust the team size or time commitment in an activity. Any of the activities can become more in-depth when you consider organizational examples, knowledge, and practice time. It is recommended that you spend the minimum suggested time allotted to get the most out of the activities.

- Notify participants. Send an invitation message to participants with details about the date, time, and location of the session. Tell them that the purpose is to introduce them to The Five Practices of Exemplary Leadership® or to deepen their leadership knowledge and skill.

- Arrange for the room and equipment you will need. Select a room in which participants will be comfortable and unlikely to be disturbed. These activities are designed to encourage interaction, so set the room up with tables arranged so that participants can easily see you, any materials or flip charts, and each other. On the day of the session, arrive early enough to make sure that the room is set up properly and the equipment is in working order.

- Practice facilitating the activity. Walk through the activity until you are comfortable with the material, facilitating the activities, and so on.

- Another suggestion to make the most of these activities is to have participants choose "commitment partners." These partnerships are designed to give each participant a sounding board outside of the classroom to obtain feedback on how he or she is doing and what he or she might do differently. For example, commitment partners could be assigned at least one follow-up meeting after each activity, in which they would discuss specific questions or activities appropriate to your organization. The partnerships could be formed at the beginning of the first The Leadership Challenge Values Card activity for the group and last through all of the activities, or the make-up of the partnerships could change from one activity to the next. Considerations in choosing commitment partners include:

- *Location:* Would it be beneficial for partners to be in the same location, or would you prefer to leverage relationships across locations?
- *Department:* Are all participants from the same department? If not, how will you pair people? By department or across departments?
- *Familiarity:* Would partners who know each other well be paired up, or would you prefer to expand participants' relationships by pairing up those who are less well acquainted?
- *Frequency:* How frequently would you expect partners to meet or talk? Does that impact any of the other considerations listed?
- *Commitment:* Will partners commit to themselves only, or will you formalize the partnerships and create a reporting mechanism for them to report back to the group and/or facilitator?

During the Session

Here are some suggestions to keep the activities on track during the session:

- *Watch the time.* The times given in this Facilitator's Guide are estimates. Keep things moving. Bring discussions and activities to a close when time is up.

- *Manage discussions.* Keep discussions focused on the topic at hand. If participants veer off topic, bring them back. If they begin to repeat themselves, summarize the discussion and move on to the next topic.
- *Encourage participants to contribute their own stories.* The more participants can relate the content of an activity to their own experiences and situations, the more useful the time will be to them. Encourage them to share their own experiences and discuss ways the concepts relate to their organizations.

Follow-Up

Many activities will include suggested follow-ups. However, creating your own follow-ups, based on what will be successful in your organization, is encouraged. The more often the concepts are reinforced to leaders, the stronger their leadership will become. For example, you might send out *The Leadership Challenge Newsletter*, or sign-up your leaders for the newsletter (see resources below), or schedule follow-up meetings two weeks after each activity. These can be brief, but they will go a long way in reinforcing what leaders have learned since the activity.

SUCCESSFUL RESULTS

The best way to become familiar with this Facilitator's Guide is to start to use the activities with leaders in your organization. By preparing for and delivering the activities, you will understand what works for you and your leaders, as well as areas in which you might want to customize them for your organization. You may also want to follow up with those who have participated in the activities. By following up with participants, you can obtain feedback on the activities, as well as hear how their leadership behaviors have changed or improved.

ADDITIONAL RESOURCES

James M. Kouzes and Barry Z. Posner. *The Leadership Challenge* (4th ed.) San Francisco: Jossey-Bass, 2007.

The Leadership Challenge Website (www.leadershipchallenge.com) offers a number of introductory articles, including the following website headings:

- "About *The Leadership Challenge*" includes the history of TLC, the approach, and video interviews of the authors.
- "Research" includes research by the authors, as well as hundreds of other research papers using the *Leadership Practices Inventory* as a tool for measurement.
- "Expand Your Skills" includes a section on "Tips & Techniques" for using the five practices.
- "Ask the Expert," which has common questions answered by experts on *The Leadership Challenge*. "Recommended Reading" and the *TLC Newsletter* are also housed under this heading.

INTRODUCTORY ACTIVITIES

Activity 1: Values Matter Board Game

Activity 2: Leader Tell Us . . . *

ACTIVITY 1
VALUES MATTER
BOARD GAME

ACTIVITY OVERVIEW

Participants use the Values cards and "Values Matter" scenarios to play a fun and lively game for building knowledge of how values impact individuals and organizations.

PURPOSE

The purpose of this activity is to provide an opportunity to learn more about how values impact individuals and organizations in a fun way. As a result of this activity, participants will be able to:

• Identify how values impact personal as well as the organizational success.

PARTICIPANTS

Minimum: 2 per game board
Maximum: 5 per game board
Recommended: 3 to 5 per game board
(Participants are divided into groups/teams of three to five. Avoid forming teams larger than five members to maintain the timing of the game.)

PREREQUISITES

None

TIME

45 to 60 minutes, including setup, the activity, and a debriefing

SUPPLIES AND RESOURCES

- The Leadership Challenge Values Card deck for each group (one or two decks, depending on Variation)
- Values Matter Board Game for each group
- Values Matter Cards and Game Pieces for each group
- One die for each group (not included)
- The Leadership Practices and Commitments handout (number 1) for each participant
- The Leadership Challenge Values Card deck for each participant to take away

FACILITATOR NOTES

Activity Setup
- Divide participants into equal-sized groups of three to five members each. Seat group members around a table.
- Distribute Values Matter Board Game, The Leadership Challenge Values Cards, Values Matter Cards, colored game pieces for each participant, and one die to each group.

Overview
(Note: If participants have not yet been introduced to The Leadership Challenge, provide a brief overview and distribute the Leadership Practices and Commitments handout to each participant. Refer to the Introduction to this Facilitator's Guide for a general introduction, adding your own experience and understanding.)

Say something like the following:

Kouzes and Posner believe, and research shows, that personal values drive commitment and shared values make a difference. Knowing what really matters to leaders is critical to leadership and success in an organization.

Today we will begin to learn more about how values impact organizations and individuals through a board game. The purpose of this activity is to provide an opportunity to learn more about values in a fun way. As a result of this activity, you will be able to identify how values impact personal as well as organizational success.

Introduce the Activity

Review the following instructions before beginning play.

- *The object of the game is for you to move your game piece on the game board by discussing how values impact both personal and organizational success. The first player to reach "finish" wins the game.*
- *Each player will choose a game piece (marked Leaders 1 through 5) and place it on "Start." Each player will roll the die to decide who goes first. The game will then rotate to the first player's left. The The Leadership Challenge Values Cards and the Values Matter Cards should be shuffled and set face down to the side of the game board.*
- *The game will take about forty-five minutes to play, so let's get started!*

Play the Game

1. The first player rolls the die. The player to his/her right draws a The Leadership Challenge Value Card, reads the **value** aloud. The first player then states why this value is important for him/her personally or for the organization. There are no right answers, only discussions; however, if a player cannot comment on the importance of the value, other players can challenge that person (see step 2).
2. If the first player cannot describe the importance of the value, other players may answer. Start with the player to the first player's left. If the second player can answer the question,

the player moves his/her game piece ahead on the game board the number of spaces on the die. The original player moves back one space.

3. The The Leadership Challenge Value Card is moved to the bottom of the deck and the game rotates to the next player on the left.

4. The Values Matter Cards are used when a player lands on a star. Then person to his/her right draws one Values Matter Card. These cards have questions and answers about the importance of values (true/false, multiple-choice, or open-ended questions). The person to the player's right reads the question on the card aloud (not the answer!). The player answers the question and then, after hearing the correct answer, either moves back or ahead as instructed. Here is an example: Number 8. True or False: Your words and actions do not demonstrate what you value as a leader. (Answer = False: They do!) Move ahead three spaces if correct, back three spaces if incorrect.

Complete the Activity

After reviewing the rules and the flow of the game, practice the game with one The Leadership Challenge Values Card, without anyone receiving points. Once everyone is clear on the rules, allow each group to complete the game to identify a winner.

Debrief

Ask participants the following questions, and probe for more information when necessary:

- *Who are the winners at each table? (Have participants give the winners a round of applause!)*
- *No matter who won, the object of this game was to help you learn the importance of values.*

- *What have we learned about how values relate to your personal leadership?*
- *What have we learned about how values relate to organizational leadership?*
- *How can you apply what you learned today about values to some real leadership situations you are facing?*

Wrap Up

As we noted when we began, leadership is learned. Understanding values is critical for leaders to Model the Way.

Our game today helped you learn more about how individuals and organizations apply values. You should be more comfortable now identifying why values matter. As you move ahead, look for leadership opportunities to apply what you learned today.

Thank the group for their participation.

COACH'S NOTES

If you are working one-on-one with a leader, you can adapt this activity. While the game board may not be best suited for coaching a leader, you might use the Values Matter Cards to prompt discussion and to help the leader become more familiar with the importance of values in leadership.

You might also have the leader share similar situations that he/she has been in and discuss how he/she used values to address those situations.

HANDOUT 1
THE LEADERSHIP PRACTICES AND COMMITMENTS

Model the Way

1. Clarify values by finding your voice and affirming shared ideals.

2. Set the example by aligning actions and shared values.

Inspire a Shared Vision

3. Envision the future by imagining exciting and ennobling possibilities.

4. Enlist others in a common vision by appealing to shared aspirations.

Challenge the Process

5. Search for opportunities by seizing the initiative and by looking outward for innovative ways to improve.

6. Experiment and take risks by constantly generating small wins and learning from experience.

Enable Others to Act

7. Foster collaboration by building trust and facilitating relationships.

8. Strengthen others by increasing self-determination and developing competence.

Encourage the Heart

9. Recognize contributions by showing appreciation for individual excellence.

10. Celebrate the values and victories by creating a spirit of community.

The Leadership Challenge Values Cards
Copyright © 2010 by James M. Kouzes and Barry Z. Posner.
Reproduced by permission of Pfeiffer, an Imprint of Wiley. www.pfeiffer.com

ACTIVITY 2
LEADERS TELL US . . .*

ACTIVITY OVERVIEW

This is a drawing game, similar to Win, Lose, or Draw and Pictionary. Participants use the The Leadership Challenge Values Cards to pick values that they will draw for their teams. Teams that guess correctly win points while learning more about values leaders use to guide their actions and decisions.

PURPOSE

The purpose of this activity is to provide an opportunity to learn how we define "values" in a fun way and practice creating visual imagery, which is key for Inspiring a Shared Vision.

As a result of this activity, participants will be able to:

- Identify a number of commonly shared values in the The Leadership Challenge Values Card decks.
- Illustrate the values in a visual way.

PARTICIPANTS

Minimum: 4
Maximum: 40
Recommended: 10 to 14
    (Participants are divided into two to four groups)

PREREQUISITES

None

Adapted from an activity originally implemented by Jim Kouzes and Barry Posner.

TIME

30 to 60 minutes (depending on time available), including setup, the activity, and the debriefing

SUPPLIES AND RESOURCES

- The Leadership Challenge Values Card deck for each group
- The Leadership Challenge Values Card deck per person for Variation 1
- Leaders Tell Us . . . Scoring Sheet
- Die, timer, pencil, and flip-chart markers for each group (not provided)
- Also needed are large sheets of paper and/or easel pads and masking tape
- The Leadership Practices and Commitments handout (number 1) for each participant

FACILITATOR NOTES

Activity Setup

- Form two teams by dividing players into teams of equal number. If there are more than twenty people playing, form three teams. Form four teams with thirty-one to forty people playing. Ideally, each team will have fewer than ten participants.
- Distribute a timer, markers, and deck of The Leadership Challenge Values Cards to each team.

Overview

(Note: If participants have not yet been introduced to The Leadership Challenge, provide a brief overview. Refer to the Introduction to this Facilitator's Guide for a general introduction, adding your own experience and understanding. You may also want to provide The Leadership Practices and Commitments Handout as a visual reminder.)

Share with participants:

Today we will begin to explore values through a game. The purpose of this activity is to provide an opportunity to learn how we define "values" in a fun way and practice creating visual imagery, which is key for Inspiring a Shared Vision. As a result of this activity, you will be able to identify a number of commonly shared values in the The Leadership Challenge Values Card decks and illustrate the values in a visual way.

Introduce the Activity

Review the following instructions before beginning play.

- High die roll decides which team plays first. The first team selects a Lead Drawer; all other first team players are then the Guessers. As one team draws and guesses the word(s) on the The Leadership Challenge Values Card, the opposing team watches. Play alternates between teams with each new phrase to be drawn.
- Rotate the role of Lead Drawer on a team so that all team members have the opportunity to be the Lead Drawer.

Play the game.

1. The Lead Drawer secretly looks at the first card in the game deck. It is always this person who removes the card from the game deck and sketches it for his/her team. On each game card is a value, for example, "Curiosity."
2. The Lead Drawer turns over the timer and the countdown (three minutes) begins. This is the time limit, kept track of by the opposing team.
3. The Lead Drawer then sketches out a picture clue or clues of the value on the card.

4. As the Lead Drawer sketches, her/his teammates start shouting out what they think is being drawn. Players can guess as many times as they want. Guessing is not done in turn!

5. Drawing Rules:
   - Focus on the key .concept of the value.
   - No letters, words, or numbers can be drawn. Symbols such as dollar signs ($), arrows (>), etc., are acceptable.
   - If part of the value is guessed correctly, you may write that word next to your sketch.
   - Never speak while drawing, but you may gesture to indicate whether the guess is close or off-track.
   - You may also draw an ear (a pull on your ear) to mean "sounds like" and then draw a rhyming word.
   - You may draw one or two dashes (—) to indicate how many words are in the value stated on your card (usually only one). Draw vertical lines through the dash(es) to indicate the number of syllables in the word(s) (e.g., –/–/– for lead-er-ship). See Figure 2.1 for an example.

6. Scoring:
   - *If the Lead Drawer's team guesses correctly before* the time has elapsed, this team receives 1 point and marks the score on the scoring sheet.
   - *If the Lead Drawer's team does not guess correctly* before the time is elapsed, the team does not earn a point. The second team then has ten seconds to make one guess to win 1 point. (This opportunity continues in turn until all remaining teams have made one guess.) If the opposing team does guess correctly, they receive 1 point.

   Once the point has been awarded, the next team selects a new Lead Drawer and play begins again.

FIGURE 2.1. Sample Drawing: Curiosity

Value: _Curiosity_

__/__/__/__/__ (syllables)

? ? ? ?

curiosity

cat

Complete the Activity

After reviewing the rules and the flow of the game, begin play. Play as many rounds as your allotted time will permit. At the end of the game, the team with the most points wins.

Debrief

Ask participants the following questions, and probe for more information when necessary:

- *What did you learn about values?*
- *Was it difficult or easy to draw these values? Why or Why not?*

Wrap Up

The purpose of this activity was to provide an opportunity to learn more about values in a fun way and practice creating visual imagery, which is key for Inspire a Shared Vision. Now you can identify a number of values, and you may even have a better sense of what values you hold. Thinking about them through pictures is a great way for you to recall them as you develop and practice your own values. Having the values "top-of-mind" will allow you to focus your actions on the values you find most important, and therefore improve your leadership skills.

Thank the group for their participation.

VARIATIONS

1. **Learning Aid:** Many of the values are conceptual and may be hard for some to draw. You may want to allow each participant to use the Values Card decks as resources as they are guessing. This requires one The Leadership Challenge Values Card deck per person.

2. **Individual Play:** Playing individually, rather than in a team, is a good solution if you have a small number of participants. In this variation, you can play with two to four participants. Each participant is a team.
   - First have participants write the individuals' names in the first row of the Leaders Tell Us . . . Scoring Sheet. For example, Steve would be listed in the space with Team 1, Kristen with Team 2, etc.
   - The drawing player draws for all others to guess.
   - When someone guesses the clue correctly, both the drawer and the guesser mark 1 point in the corresponding spaces. If no one guesses the clue, no points are given.
   - The player with the most points at the end of the game wins.

3. **Independent Drawing:** A third option is to have participants work independently for ten minutes to draw a visual representation of the value on cards that they pull from the deck.
   - Provide a sheet of flip-chart paper, markers, and masking tape to each participant.

- Have each participant draw from the The Leadership Challenge Values Card deck and allow ten to fifteen minutes for them to draw the value on the bottom two-thirds of the chart paper.
- After each person has competed his/her drawing, post the flip charts around the room and allow participants to go around the room to try to identify which value has been drawn on each page. Have them write their guesses with their names on the top third of the flip-chart page, allowing room for other guesses. (Amount of time allowed will vary by the number of participants.)
- Have participants return to where their own drawings are and share which value was depicted in their drawings.
- Track who had the most correct guesses to determine the winner.

COACH'S NOTES

If you are working one-on-one with a leader, you can adapt this activity in a number of ways. While there is obviously no need to keep points, this activity provides the leader with visual reminders of the values that he/she creates. For many leaders, Inspire a Shared Vision is the lowest among The Five Practices, and the most difficult to impact. Since Inspire is all about "painting the picture," this would be an excellent way to practice Inspire while focusing on his/her own Values!

One Value Per Session: You may decide to select only one card per session to draw and conduct this activity after the Values Card Sort (Activity 3), focusing on one of their five values in each session. Assigning the drawing as pre-work to your coaching session is a good idea to allow reflection time. (You may want to specify whether you prefer a large drawing on flip-chart paper or a drawing on a blank piece of 8½-by-11-inch paper.)

Have the leader post his/her drawing in his/her work area. You may want to make a copy of the drawing for your records as well.

LEADERS TELL US . . . SCORING SHEET

Scoring for Team Play

1. Write the names of the players on each team in the areas provided.

2. If the drawing team guesses correctly before the time has elapsed, the team earns 1 point and marks it in the space that corresponds to the current round. Each team repeats this step throughout each round.

3. If the drawing team does not guess correctly, each other team, in succession, has 10 seconds to guess. The first team to guess correctly earns the point.

Scoring for Individual Play

1. If playing with two to four individuals instead of in a team, write the *individuals'* names in the first row. For example, Steve would be listed in the space with Team 1, Kristen with Team 2, etc.

2. The drawing player draws for all others to guess. When someone guesses the clue correctly, both the drawer and the guesser mark 1 point in the corresponding space. If no one guesses the clue correctly, no points are given.

Name:				
Round	**Team 1 Team Member Names:***	**Team 2 Team Member Names:***	**Team 3 Team Member Names:***	**Team 4 Team Member Names:***
1				
2				
3				
4				
5				
6				
7				
8				
Total Scores:				

* Optional

HANDOUT 1 THE LEADERSHIP PRACTICES AND COMMITMENTS

Model the Way

1. Clarify values by finding your voice and affirming shared ideals.

2. Set the example by aligning actions and shared values.

Inspire a Shared Vision

3. Envision the future by imagining exciting and ennobling possibilities.

4. Enlist others in a common vision by appealing to shared aspirations.

Challenge the Process

5. Search for opportunities by seizing the initiative and by looking outward for innovative ways to improve.

6. Experiment and take risks by constantly generating small wins and learning from experience.

Enable Others to Act

7. Foster collaboration by building trust and facilitating relationships.

8. Strengthen others by increasing self-determination and developing competence.

Encourage the Heart

9. Recognize contributions by showing appreciation for individual excellence.

10. Celebrate the values and victories by creating a spirit of community.

Handouts/Materials

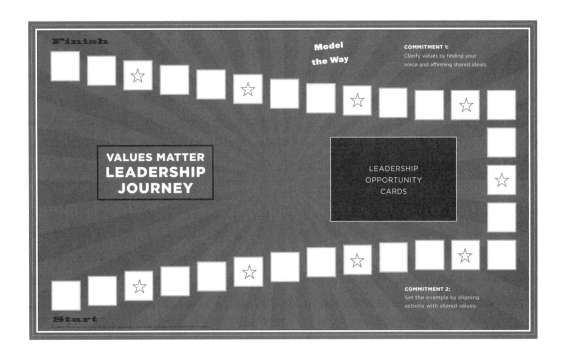

Values Matter Cards

Print one to five copies of this document on card stock, depending on the number of teams you have. Cut out the cards, shuffle, and place on the Game Board.

1. True or False: Employees are most loyal when they are focused on organizational values. **Move forward 2 spaces if correct, back 2 spaces if incorrect.**	**2.** Research shows that _____ improves in an organization where values are aligned: **(a)** employee benefits **(b)** creativity or **(c)** marketing **Move ahead 4 spaces if correct, back 4 if incorrect.**
3. . Research shows that organizations with strong values experience ____ times more growth in net income than others do: **(a)** 4 **(b)** 8 **(c)** 10 **Move forward 2 spaces if correct, back 2 spaces if incorrect.**	**4.** Research shows that organizations with strong values experience ____ times the growth in job creation compared with others: **(a)** 3 **(b)** 7 **(c)** 13 **Move forward 2 spaces if correct, back 2 spaces if incorrect.**
5. True or False: When leaders seek consensus about shared values, people are more positive. **Move forward 3 spaces if correct, back 3 spaces if incorrect.**	**6. True or False**: Clarifying your personal values has an impact on your company. **Move forward 2 spaces if correct, back 2 spaces if incorrect.**
7. . Answer the following question: Why do you think personal values impact the organization? **Move forward 4 spaces.**	**8. True or False**: Your words and actions do not demonstrate what you value as a leader. **Move ahead 3 spaces if correct, back 3 spaces if incorrect.**

Values Matter Cards

Print one to five copies of this document on card stock, depending on the number of teams you have. Cut out the cards, shuffle, and place on the Game Board.

9. Values are **(a)** empowering **(b)** motivating, **(c)** guides to action, **(d)** all of the above. **Move ahead 2 spaces if correct, back 2 spaces if incorrect.**	**10.** Which is most important to commitment to an organization? Clarity of personal or organizational values? **Move ahead 4 spaces if correct, back 4 spaces if incorrect.**
11. True or false: Research shows that successful companies have very similar values. **Move forward 3 spaces if correct, back 5 spaces if incorrect.**	**12.** "How would you like to be remembered tonight?" is a reflection question Kouzes and Posner ask. How would you answer this question? **Move ahead 3 spaces.**
13. Organizations with shared values have all of the following EXCEPT higher employee turnover rates, consensus on goals, ethical behavior, reduced level of stress. **Move forward 3 spaces if correct, move back if incorrect.**	**14. True or false**: Organizational values are most effective when chosen by a trusted company founder. **Move ahead 2 spaces if you are correct, back 2 if incorrect.**

Game Pieces

Print one to five copies of this document, depending on the number of teams you have. Cut out the game pieces and distribute to the players.

PERSONAL VALUES DRIVE COMMITMENT ACTIVITIES

Activity 3: Values Card Sort*

Activity 4: Aligning Actions with Values*

Activity 5: Are My Actions Aligned?

Activity 6: Values and Individual Interactions: How Values
Influence Our Interactions

Activity 7: Case Studies: Values as Coaching Tools

Activity 8: Your Challenging Situation: Values as Coaching Tools

ACTIVITY 3
VALUES CARD SORT*

ACTIVITY OVERVIEW

In this activity, participants review and select those values that are most important to them, thereby clarifying their personal values.

PURPOSE

To help participants address part of Commitment One (Clarify Values), as part of Model the Way, by clarifying their personal values. As a result of this activity, participants will be able to:

- State their top five values.
- Define what each of their top five values means to them.

PARTICIPANTS

Minimum: 1
Maximum: 40
Best: 12 to 15
    (Participants work on their own in this activity.)

PREREQUISITES

None

TIME

20 to 45 minutes

---

* Adapted from The Leadership Challenge® Workshop (3rd ed.).

SUPPLIES AND RESOURCES

- The Leadership Challenge Values Card decks for each participant
- Defining Your Values handout (number 2)
- Pens or pencils

FACILITATOR NOTES

Overview

Personal values have a significant impact on one's commitment to an organization. Organizations that spend time focused on helping individuals understand their own values show high levels of commitment, as shown In Figure 3.1.

Today we will look at how to address part of Commitment One (Clarify Values), as part of Model the Way, by clarifying personal values. As a result of this activity, participants will be able to state their top five values and define what each of the top five values means to them.

Activity Setup

(Note: before this activity, have the Values Card decks ready to hand out to participants.)

Explain that the best leaders have developed clarity about the core personal values that most guide them. Make these points:

- *Being clear on your personal values enables you to have more commitment to an organization.*
- *Credibility comes from consistency between what you say and what you do; therefore, you need to be clear on and believe in the values you say you live by.*
- *For the next few minutes you will have the opportunity to reflect on and better clarify the values that you hold most deeply.*

FIGURE 3.1. The Impact of Values Clarity on Commitment

Clarity of Organizational values

	Low	High
High	4.87	**6.26**
Low	4.90	6.12

Low   High

Clarity of Personal values

Level of Commitment
Scale: 1—Low
7—High

Begin the Activity

Hand out a set of Values Cards to each participant.

Review the instructions for Step 1.

Participants are to divide the cards into three piles (write these categories on a flip chart):

- Values that are *Extremely Important* to you
- Values that are *Moderately Important* to you
- Values that are *Not Important* to you

Participants may ask, "Are these my values at work or at home?" Explain that the strongest leaders are consistent in their values in all aspects of their lives.

Allow time for all participants to sort their cards into three piles.

(Note: If possible, allow each participant to take his/her time sorting the cards. Some may take a good deal of time—up to thirty minutes—in this part of the exercise. If time is short, allow at least fifteen minutes for this part of the exercise.)

Review the instructions for Step 2.

Once all participants have three piles, ask them how many cards they have in each pile. You'll often find many cards in Extremely Important and Important.

Now ask them to take the cards that are in the Important and Not Important piles and put them aside in the card box.
Instruct participants to:

• *Focus on the pile of values you've selected that are extremely important to you. Select the FIVE most important values.*

(Note: Participants will often ask whether they can have more than five values. Emphasize that having more than five values is difficult to manage. If, for example, you had ten values, you may find yourself compromising some of your values for those that are most important to you. Five values is the ideal. There may be values that are in their top five to seven values that are similar and could be grouped. The new categories can be written on the blank cards provided in the deck.

Review the instructions for Step 3.

Once all participants have five values, have them write those values on the Defining Your Values handout. Have them create definitions for what they mean by each value, as demonstrated on the handout. Share the example from the handout: "Creativity is to be inventive and original."

Review the instructions for Step 4.

Depending on time available, you might have participants find partners to share their values and definitions, or if you have time and/or a small team, you may want to have each member share with the entire group.

Remind participants that this activity is about clarifying their personal values. If others are not clear about a participant's values, help the person clarify them by saying something like "I'm not yet clear on what you mean by this value and why it's important to you. Please say more."

Give participants ten to fifteen minutes for this activity if they are in pairs. When you are finished with Step 4, debrief the experience.

Debrief

Ask participants the following questions, and probe for more information when necessary:

- *What did you discover from this process?*
  (Possible responses: It was helpful to validate my values; I never realized how hard it is to decide which of my values are the most important; Some of my values seem to conflict with one another.)
- *What were some of the similar values?*
  (Possible responses: family; honesty/integrity; faith, etc.)
- *Why do you think it helps to learn that the values of others are different than yours?*
  (Possible responses: It helps explain how we are different individuals and have different viewpoints; It helps us to understand why someone believes what he or she believes and acts how he or she acts.)

Wrap Up

Share with participants:

- *More clarity enables leaders to better and more confidently express their beliefs, so others know what those leaders stand for.*
- *Remember, to be credible, you must first SAY what you will do and then do it!*

Thank the group for their participation.

VARIATIONS

1. **Group Values:** If time permits, participants can share their values and chart them over several flip-chart pages. Or, after they share in pairs or small groups, ask them what values they heard that were common. For example, "Honesty/Integrity" is a common value. The facilitator can write these on a flip chart as the groups report out. This creates a short, but impactful, activity that demonstrates commonalities. You might also ask what values were NOT similar. Share that these are what make us unique, and how these can help us interact together more effectively. (See Activity 9 for a full Leader's Guide to this activity.)

2. **Human Billboard:** An additional activity is to have participants create a "human billboard" on which they communicate their values using visual symbols. Each participant receives one page of flip-chart paper and draws one or all of his/her values on the page, based on the amount of time available.

COACH'S NOTES

If you are working one-on-one with a leader, you can adapt this activity. You can walk the leader through the process as explained above. Have the leader write down the definition of each of his/her values. Note that someone else with the same value may define it differently. The goal is to help define the importance of the value to that leader.

In future sessions with the leader, you can further discuss how these values are evident (or not evident) in his/her leadership behaviors.

HANDOUT 2
DEFINING YOUR VALUES

Directions: In the spaces provided below, record the top five values that you selected in the Values Card Sort activity. Define what each value means to you underneath that value. A sample has been provided.

Sample
Creativity
To be inventive and original

The Leadership Challenge Values Cards
Copyright © 2010 by James M. Kouzes and Barry Z. Posner.
Reproduced by permission of Pfeiffer, an Imprint of Wiley. www.pfeiffer.com

ACTIVITY 4
ALIGNING ACTIONS
WITH VALUES*

ACTIVITY OVERVIEW

In this activity, participants review their personal values and plan actions that can help them align their behaviors to their values.

PURPOSE

To provide the opportunity for participants to determine specific actions they can take to model the values they profess. As a result of this activity, participants will be able to:

• Take specific actions to demonstrate their values and Do What They Say They Will Do (DWTSTWD).

PARTICIPANTS

Minimum: 1
Maximum: 40
Best: 12 to 15
   (Participants work on their own or in groups of four or five people for this activity.)

PREREQUISITES

Values Card Sort (Activity 3)

---

* Adapted from The Leadership Challenge© Workshop (3rd ed.).

45

TIME

30 to 40 minutes for Group Activity, 60 minutes if Individual Activity is added

SUPPLIES AND RESOURCES

- Completed list of top five values from Defining Your Values (Handout 2 from Activity 3) for each participant
- Blank copies of Defining Your Values handout (number 2) for participants for either the Individual or the Group Activity
- Values in Action Worksheet (Handout 3) for each participant
- Flip-chart paper and easel for each group
- Markers

FACILITATOR NOTES

Activity Setup

- Divide participants into table groups of four or five. Explain that participants will work in small groups to identify actions they can take to model their leadership behaviors. For this activity, each group will need access to an easel with flip-chart paper and markers.

Overview

Explain that credibility comes from doing what you say you will do. Make these points:

- *The well-known scholar of leadership John Gardner once said the goal is not to continually seek better values, but to live the ones we profess.*
- *Leaders take stands on values and demonstrate their commitment to those values through visible actions.*
- *Credibility comes from doing what you say. As a leader, your effectiveness is judged on what you do. For example, leaders*

may talk about quality; they make quality real by publicly supporting, congratulating, and rewarding those whose work lives up to the standards.

Introduce the Activity

Share with participants that there are many ways that they can take specific, visible actions to model their values.

For example, if a leader's value is "teamwork," you would see that leader demonstrate the value if he/she ensures that the team meets to discuss critical issues or if he/she encourages team members to seek out others to gain additional input. Another example is "honesty." If a leader has a value of honesty, he/she provides information and shares (within reason) his/her thoughts. For example, a leader may say, "I'll tell you what I know, find out, or let you know that I have information but cannot share it" in order to be as transparent as possible.

Ask participants for other examples of things leaders can do to demonstrate their values. Elicit a few responses and write them on a flip-chart page.

Briefly review each of the six ways in which leaders set the example and demonstrate their commitment to shared values. They are

- Calendars
- Critical Incidents
- Stories
- Language
- Measurements
- Rewards

Hand out the Values in Action Worksheet.

Ask participants to take a couple of minutes to read each of the descriptions on the Values in Action Worksheet. Then briefly explain some of the categories. For example:

- *Calendars—You need to be aware of how you spend your time. If you preach the importance of customer relationships, how much time do you actually spend with customers? If you say you value developing your people, how much time do you actually spend talking with individuals about their progress and development needs, as opposed to focusing on financial reports and other financial tasks?*
- *Stories—Ever hear people say, "And the moral of the story is . . . ?" Stories are colorful ways to teach people about values. If you think it's important to produce quality products, tell a story about how an employee stopped the assembly line because defective products were being produced, fixed the problem, and enabled the company to retain its record of near-perfect quality.*
- *Rewards—To what extent do you recognize and reward people for upholding the values you believe in? Do you only recognize people for financial results or do you reward them for things like being collaborative with colleagues or honest with customers in tough situations? In other words, for practicing the values that you say are important?*
- *Measurement—Measuring how others live a specific value sounds difficult, right? How do you measure Honesty, for example. There are ways to both set informal and formal measurements. If Teamwork is a value, you can look at how often people are working together on a project, or whether they work more often alone. When you challenge yourself to come up with measurements for your values, you will have valuable feedback on how your actions are aligned.*

Explain that participants will work in small groups to identify actions they can take to model their values.

(Note: For the following activity, each group will need access to an easel with a flip-chart page and markers.)

Group Activity

Form small groups (four to five people).

1. Ask each group to select a value one of the group members identified during the Values Card Sort (see Defining Your Values handout completed during Activity 3).
2. Give the groups three to five minutes to brainstorm some actions they can take to model the value they selected, using the categories listed on their worksheets. These may be actions that are currently being done, suggestions or new ideas, or current activities that should be stopped. Explain that they do not have to have responses for every category, and that they can add a new category if they wish.
3. Ask participants to record their responses from the Values in Action worksheets onto a flip-chart page.
4. When time is up, ask groups to post their flip-chart pages where the entire group can see them. Ask everyone to walk around the room and review the posted responses. Suggest that participants write down any of the other groups' suggestions that appeal to them, asking for clarification.

OPTION: If you are short on time, you can skip Step 4, or even have each individual work on his/her own rather than in a group (see Variations below). Then ask each group or individual to share one or two examples of the value he/she selected and the responses he/she wrote on the worksheet.

Remind participants that the purpose of the previous activity was to get them thinking about how to connect actions with values. Explain that you will now give them a few minutes to select values that are important to them, reflect on them, and identify some ways they can live the value more frequently.

Individual Activity

Ask participants to turn to the blank Values in Action Worksheet. Give them four to five minutes to do the following:

1. Select a value that is important to them, preferably a different value than the one they worked on in small groups. Write the value at the top of the worksheet.
2. Complete the worksheet by indicating what they can do in the different categories to model that value. They do not have to have responses for each category, and they can add a new category if they wish.
3. When they have completed their worksheets, have participants find partners with whom they can share their responses and gain additional suggestions.

Debrief

Ask participants the following questions, and probe for more information when necessary:

- *How easy is it to come up with actions to demonstrate commitment to values?*

  (Possible responses: There are a lot of things people can do; the hard part is following through on those actions consistently; you cannot do one action a week and expect people to view you differently, etc.)

- *What will it take for you to ensure that you follow through and act in ways consistent with your shared values? What if two of your values are in conflict? (for example, achievement and success, harmony)*
  (Possible responses: Schedule these actions into your week; set aside time in staff meetings for recognition or to institute "moments of truth"—great examples of someone on the team demonstrating a value, etc.)

Wrap Up

Share with participants:

- *DWYSYWD (Do What You Say You Will Do) has a great impact on your credibility. It is a mantra that you want to take away from Model the Way by demonstrating your values in everyday actions.*

Thank the group for their participation.

VARIATIONS

1. **Saving Time:** If you are short on time, you can skip Step 4 of the Group Activity, or even have each individual work on his/her own rather than in a group (see Individual Activity instructions). Then ask each group or individual to share one or two examples of the value selected and the responses from the worksheet.

2. **Movie Discussion:** This is a fun way to generate discussion about how values and actions align, either as an introduction or as a wrap-up to the activities above. Show the preview of a movie in which a character receives supernatural powers to help

others, but ends up using the powers for his/her own good. Use the following questions to debrief the preview:

- How should the character have utilized his/her supernatural power?
- How did he/she act instead?
- What did he/she do, and what values do you think that demonstrated?
- Who has seen the movie, and what were the outcomes?

3. **Role Play:** Allowing leaders to role play using their values provides a way for leaders to practice in a controlled environment. Speaking the words they would use to align the values and actions prepares them to demonstrate the values and provides a great learning opportunity. To create a role play, follow the steps below.

- Logistics:
  - The ideal number of participants per group is three. This allows each person to play the role of leader.
  - This will add approximately thirty minutes per leader or ninety minutes overall.
- Have participants select who will go first, second, and third in leading their own role plays. As each role play begins, non-leaders will play the other characters in the scenario based on the instruction by the leader. For example, in Role Play 1, there will be a leader and participants playing two roles chosen by the leader (perhaps two direct reports or a colleague and an observer). If there are more participants than roles, ask the remaining people to observe and take notes.
- Using the notes they have taken about which values they'd use and how, the leader will address the other characters regarding the issue. Allow approximately five minutes for

the leaders to write a few bullet points for how they would approach the issue.

- Create the following flip chart to provide direction:

---

1. Get into groups of three people.

2. Choose leaders:
   - Role Play 1 (Leader 1): _____
   - Role Play 2 (Leader 2): _____
   - Role Play 3 (Leader 3): _____

3. Leaders all spend five minutes; list bullet points on what you will say.

4. Role Play 1: What are the roles and who will play them? Observer?

5. Conduct the role play: ten minutes.

6. Give feedback: ten minutes.

7. Switch to next role play: switch leaders, characters

- Conduct the role play and allow time for feedback to the leaders about how well they used the appropriate leadership behaviors.
- Debrief by asking the following questions:
   - *What did you learn about demonstrating the value you chose?*
   - *What was difficult about the role play?*
   - *What did you see as observers or other characters that was done effectively by the leaders?*
   - *As leaders, what did you think you could have done better?*
   - *How will what you have learned help you with the situation you addressed?*
   - *How will this role-play activity impact the way that you demonstrate your values in your daily work?*

COACH'S NOTES

If you are working one-on-one with a leader, you can adapt this activity. First, work together with the leader to complete the Group Activity by determining several actions you can take to align activities around one value—perhaps an organizational value or a general value that many share. This will generate ideas that can be applied to another important value that the leader would like to demonstrate in his/her leadership. Once you've completed the Group Activity, the leader may complete the Individual Activity on his/her own. Debrief the activity together, suggesting additional ways that the leader could demonstrate the value as needed.

On an ongoing basis, use this activity to help the leader "check in" on how his/her actions and behaviors are aligned with the values that he/she espouses. Discuss the impact of his/her leadership on others.

HANDOUT 2
DEFINING YOUR VALUES

Directions: In the spaces provided below, record the top five values that you selected in the Values Card Sort activity. Define what each value means to you underneath that value. A sample has been provided.

Sample
Creativity
To be inventive and original

HANDOUT 2
DEFINING YOUR VALUES

Directions: In the spaces provided below, record the top five values that you selected in the Values Card Sort activity. Define what each value means to you underneath that value. A sample has been provided.

Sample
Creativity
To be inventive and original

The Leadership Challenge Values Cards
Copyright © 2010 by James M. Kouzes and Barry Z. Posner.
Reproduced by permission of Pfeiffer, an Imprint of Wiley. www.pfeiffer.com

HANDOUT 3
VALUES IN ACTION WORKSHEET

Calendar

You need to be aware of how you spend your time. If you preach the importance of customer relationships, how much time do you actually spend with customers? If you say you value developing your people, how much time do you actually spend talking with individuals about their progress and developmental needs, as opposed to focusing on financial reports and other financial tasks?

Critical Incidents

These significant moments of learning are often referred to as "teachable moments." Are you using unexpected occurrences to demonstrate appropriate leadership behaviors? In the case of a product recall, are you demonstrating the importance of good customer service by proactively contacting your customers and asking "What can we learn?" or are you spending time determining the effect this will have on future revenue?

Stories

Ever hear people say, "And the moral of the story is. . . ?" Stories are colorful ways to talk about leadership behaviors. If you think it's important to produce quality products, tell a story about how an employee stopped the assembly line because defective products were being produced, fixed the problem, and enabled the company to retain its record of near-perfect quality.

The Leadership Challenge Values Cards
Copyright © 2010 by James M. Kouzes and Barry Z. Posner.
Reproduced by permission of Pfeiffer, an Imprint of Wiley. www.pfeiffer.com

Language

Leaders understand the power of words, and they often choose them carefully. Metaphors and analogies can be effective for creating a vision, and the questions leaders ask often frame the issues and set the agenda. How does your choice of words illustrate the core values of the organization?

Measurements

There is a saying that "What gets measured is what gets done." Measurement and feedback are essential to improved performance. Is what you have identified as a core value what is actually being measured? If corporate community involvement is a core value, are you keeping metrics on the community service activities your staff members participate in?

Rewards

To what extent do you recognize and reward people for upholding the values you believe in? Do you only recognize people for financial results or do you reward them for things like being collaborative with colleagues or honest with customers in tough situations? In other words, for practicing the values that you say are important.

SAMPLE HANDOUT 3
VALUES IN ACTION WORKSHEET

Core Value: Customer Service
Action Ideas

Calendar

Answer customer service phones one morning per month.
Visit client site once a week.

Critical Incidents

The next time there is an unusual disruption in normal service, take on a front-line job to demonstrate that the customer comes first.

Assign specific roles for staff members to take during service disruptions and have people practice those roles.

Stories

Begin every staff meeting with customer stories, including both successes and learning opportunities.

Language

Start referring to staff members as "associates" instead of employees. Eliminate "subordinate" from your vocabulary. Eliminate "us/them" language from interdepartmental conversations.

Measurements

Conduct customer satisfaction survey.

Determine key leading indicators for your success and make them the key measures for the future.

Focus on eliminating repeat calls for customer service issues (solve the problem on the first call).

Ask, "How will it affect customers?" when advising others.

Rewards

Give company-wide bonus for improving customer satisfaction rating.

Set up an Applause! bulletin board for every location.

HANDOUT 3
VALUES IN ACTION WORKSHEET

Core Value: _____

Action Ideas

Calendar

_____

_____

_____

Critical Incidents

_____

_____

_____

Stories

_____

_____

_____

Language

_____

_____

_____

_____

Measurements

_____

_____

_____

Rewards

_____

_____

_____

_____

HANDOUT 3
VALUES IN ACTION WORKSHEET

Core Value: _____

Action Ideas

Calendar

_____

_____

_____

Critical Incidents

_____

_____

_____

Stories

_____

_____

_____

Language

_____

_____

_____

_____

Measurements

_____

_____

_____

_____

Rewards

_____

_____

_____

ACTIVITY 5
ARE MY ACTIONS ALIGNED?

ACTIVITY OVERVIEW

In this activity, team leaders review their values with their teams and ask for input on how well their actions are aligned with these values. This activity is best facilitated by a person external to the team, but can be facilitated by the leader if the team dynamics are positive.

PURPOSE

To help leaders understand how their actions are perceived and how these actions are aligned with their values. As a result of this activity, leaders will be able to:

- Solicit feedback from others on how their values and actions are aligned.
- Identify perceived gaps for which their actions are not aligned with their stated values.

PARTICIPANTS

Minimum: 2
Maximum: 15
Best: 6 to 10
  (For this activity, leaders work with their intact teams.)

PREREQUISITES

Values Card Sort (Activity 3)

TIME

90 minutes

SUPPLIES AND RESOURCES

- Completed copies of the team leader's Defining Your Values handout (Handout 2 from Activity 3) for each participant
- Flip-chart paper and easel
- Markers
- Facilitator external to the team is optional but recommended

FACILITATOR NOTES

Overview

(Note: This activity is intended to help a leader solicit feedback from his/her team regarding how his/her values and actions are aligned. Therefore, the leader introduces the activity, but it is recommended that a facilitator outside of the team lead other parts of the activity.)

If participants have not yet taken the Leadership Practices Inventory or been introduced to The Leadership Challenge, provide a brief overview. Refer to the Introduction to this Facilitator's Guide for a general introduction, adding your own experience and understanding.

Activity Setup

The leader explains that the best leaders have developed clarity about the core personal values that most guide them, and that they ensure that their actions are aligned with those values. The leaders should make the following points:

- *Leaders need to Do What You Say You Will Do—DWYSYWD.*
- *Authors Jim Kouzes and Barry Posner, in The Leadership Challenge® Workshop, pose this question: "If your team found a sheet of paper with your values on it, without your name, would they know those are your values?" And an even tougher question: "If your team found your values on a sheet of paper with your name at the top, would they agree based on the actions they see every day?"*
- *I hope that I align my actions with my values so that each is transparent to you.*
- *As a leader, I thought it would be helpful for me, as well as for us as a team, to get deeper into the questions that Kouzes and Posner pose.*

Describe the process.

- *I'll be asking you to share what actions of mine you see that demonstrate my personal values. What other things could I be doing to better demonstrate my values at work?*
- (Note: If you have an outside facilitator, explain his/her role and that you will be leaving the room in a moment. Assure the team that they can be candid. If you are facilitating the session, you will remain in the room to facilitate the discussion. A third option is to have this conversation one-on-one with team members.)

Distribute the leader's completed Defining Your Values handout.

Review what you (or he/she) wrote on your handout, defining what each value means to you and why it is so important. State that you will focus today only on those values that they can see you demonstrate at work. You can decide, as the leader, for example, whether or not you want to go in-depth about how your actions at work are aligned with such values as Faith. This will take about ten minutes.

Share the following examples:

- *So if one of my values is relationships, and you believe that I allow time for team discussion and fun to build our relationships, my actions would be aligned with that value.*
- *If, on the other hand, one of my values is honesty/integrity, and you have noticed that I don't share information with you, that might mean my actions are not aligned with my values.*

Clarify that the team understands the process and then, if the team leader is facilitating the activity, he/she leaves the room. Allow twenty to thirty minutes for discussion.

Facilitate the discussion.

The facilitator (the leader of the team or the outside facilitator) takes up to forty minutes in this step and writes each value at the top of a flip-chart page. On the right side of the page, the team will list actions that are aligned with this value, on the left, the actions that are not aligned with this value. An example is demonstrated in below.

- For each value, ask for examples of how the leader demonstrates this value, and when he/she could demonstrate it more, or differently. Ask participants to give specifics when necessary.
- The facilitator should monitor the time so that there is plenty of time to capture information for each value.

Honesty/Integrity	
Actions That Are Aligned	*Actions That Are Not Aligned*
He/she gives me honest feedback	Didn't share information about a recent change until after we found out
Is honest about his/her thoughts about the company and our team	Doesn't share that he/she has information, but it is confidential
Always does the right thing for the customer	Talks negatively about changes when they happen

Debrief

The leader returns to the room and asks the facilitator to present the results of the discussion. The leader can ask questions to clarify meanings, and the facilitator can provide input to help clarify.

(Note to the team leader: In some cases, the actions team members mention do not match with your idea of how you act regarding your defined values. It is important to not react defensively. Ask for examples to clarify actions that do not seem related to your defined values.)

You may also want to share some of the actions that you planned in Activity 4, "Aligning Actions with Values."

Share your responses and what learnings you have from the activity.

Wrap Up

Share with the group that leadership is a continuous learning process, and that your continued development relies on your deliberate practice to align your actions and values, as well as the feedback that they give you. Ask the group to continue to provide feedback when they see actions that are either aligned or not aligned with your espoused values. Set up regular "touch-base" meetings either individually or as a group to solicit additional feedback.

Let the team know that you value their input and feedback. Ask them to look for times when you are demonstrating your values and times when you could focus more on your values.

Thank the group for their participation.

VARIATIONS

1. **Focus on One or Two Values:** If time is short, focus on one or two of the most critical values. If time permits, hold several sessions to discuss each of the values individually.

2. **Two Meetings to "Digest" the Feedback:** You may want to hold the meeting in two sessions, allowing the facilitator to debrief the leader in a separate meeting. This is especially helpful if the information is more difficult or the leader has had little experience with receiving direct feedback. The facilitator can then coach the leader on his/her response for the most effective session.

COACH'S NOTES

If you are working one-on-one with a leader, you can adapt this activity. You may play the role of the facilitator or have the leader conduct the activity on his/her own or with another facilitator. If you facilitate the activity, you can coach the leader about the feedback and how to respond appropriately to his/her group.

ACTIVITY 6
VALUES AND INDIVIDUAL INTERACTIONS: HOW VALUES INFLUENCE OUR INTERACTIONS

ACTIVITY OVERVIEW

In this activity, participants examine how different values have an impact on how leaders interact with others.

PURPOSE

Provide the opportunity for participants to see how values impact our relationships so that they are better able to understand and adapt to others as leaders. As a result of this activity, participants will be able to:

- Identify how values differ and may cause conflict.
- Address differences in values in a way that builds effective communication among team members.

PARTICIPANTS

Minimum: 3
Maximum: 40
Best: 12 to 15
(Participants work pairs or in groups of three people for this activity.)

PREREQUISITES

Values Card Sort (Activity 3)

TIME

45 to 60 minutes

SUPPLIES AND RESOURCES

- The Leadership Challenge Values Card decks for each group
- Values and Individual Actions Worksheet handout (number 4) for each participant
- Flip charts and easels for each group
- Markers

FACILITATOR NOTES

Overview

As leaders, we have to recognize that people are different. People have different levels of experience, different styles, and hold different values. Leaders can help others to work effectively together by recognizing these differences and coaching others on how to address the differences. This activity provides the opportunity for participants to see how values impact our relationships so that they are better able to understand and adapt to others as leaders. As a result of this activity, participants will be able to identify how values differ and may cause conflict and address differences in values in a way that builds effective communication among team members.

Activity Setup

Explain that leaders have to adapt their leadership to those they are leading. For example, if you are leading a person who is new to the job, you adapt differently to his/her needs than you would to someone who is more tenured.

The same is true for the values that others hold. When leaders are aware of the values that team members hold, they have insight about how to lead each person.

Ask participants for examples of values that team members might have. Elicit a few responses and ask how these may complement or conflict with each other.

Describe the process of the activity:

- *In pairs or in groups of three, you will take turns drawing three cards from your Values Card decks.*
- *Once you have drawn three cards, assume that these values are associated with three people working together on a project or process.*
- *Your group will have a discussion about how three people with these three values would work together. Use the Values and Individual Actions Worksheet (Handout 4) to record your process.*
- *As a first step, discuss with your group how each of you would define the values. You'll note that there are not only variations in what we value, but in how we define each value. Take five minutes to do this.*
- Use the following questions for your discussion:
  - *What challenges might be presented if these are the three primary values of the team members?*
  - *How might they overcome these challenges?*
  - *If you were the leader of this group (they report to you or you are responsible for the project), what might you do to facilitate communication and collaboration for this group?*
  - *What if the values are similar? What challenges or benefits might this involve? How can they overcome these risks?*

Repeat the activity at least three times and then ask participants to summarize what they've learned and write their summaries on their flip charts. Ask them to be prepared to share examples as needed.

Debrief

Ask each group to share its summary; then ask the following questions:

- *When values were very different, perhaps in conflict, what were some of your ideas to lead through the project?*
  (Possible responses: Discuss values up-front with the group; talk about why the values are important; encourage people to be considerate of others.)
- *How often does this conflict of values happen in your work environment? How does it impact the work that you and your group do?*
  (Possible responses: Happened a lot before, but we didn't know it until we did the Values Cards; before I just saw people as uncooperative, but now I know they are focused on a particular value, so I work with that.)

Wrap Up

Share with participants:

- *Being aware of your values, as well as those of others, can enhance the work of any team. As leaders, you can facilitate this understanding with others and become a catalyst for success in your team!*
- *Now that you've had demonstrations about how values can differ, you can better understand and adapt to others as leaders.*

Thank the group for their participation.

VARIATIONS

1. **Save Time:** If you are short on time, have participants do only one round. Have each group share the high-level results of their discussion so that they hear other possible scenarios.

2. **Role Play:** Allowing leaders to role play using the situations created in the activity provides a way for leaders to practice in a controlled environment. Speaking the words they would use in interactions with others around values prepares them to have discussions and provides a great learning opportunity. To create a role play, follow the steps below.
   - Logistics:
     - The ideal number of participants per group is three. This allows each person to play the role of leader.
     - This will add approximately thirty minutes per leader or ninety minutes overall.
   - Have participants select who will go first, second, and third in leading their own role plays. As each role play begins, non-leaders will play the other characters in the scenario based on the instruction by the leader. For example, the first leader will lead the role playing based on the notes from Round 1. Let's say the values were "Honesty/Integrity," "Creativity," and "Achievement/ Success." The leader would pick two values and assign them to each of the two participants, who would play their roles based on the value, using each of the three rounds described above.
   - Using the notes they have taken, the leader will assume that he or she is having a discussion about the conflict in values that has arisen between the two participants. Allow approximately five minutes for the leader to write a few bullet points for how he/she would approach the issue.
   - Create the following flip chart to provide direction:

1. Get into groups of three people.
2. Choose leaders:
   - Role Play 1 (Leader 1): _____
   - Role Play 2 (Leader 2): _____
   - Role Play 3 (Leader 3): _____
3. Leaders all spend five minutes; list bullet points on what you will say.
4. Role Play 1: What are the roles and who will play them? Observer?
5. Conduct the role play: ten minutes.
6. Give feedback: ten minutes.
7. Switch to next role play: switch leaders, characters

- Conduct the role play and allow time for feedback to the leaders about how well they used the appropriate leadership behaviors.
- Debrief by asking the following questions:
  - *What did you learn about conflicting values?*
  - *What was difficult about the role play?*
  - *What did you see as observers or other characters that was done effectively by the leaders?*
  - *As leaders, what did you think you could have done better?*
  - *How will what you have learned help you with the situation you addressed?*
  - *How will this role-play activity impact the way that you demonstrate your values in your daily work?*

COACH'S NOTES

If you are working one-on-one with a leader, you can still utilize this activity as outlined for groups. You may encourage the leader to discuss actual examples of when individuals' values have differed in his/her work and the results of this. Discuss how the leader can manage those differences with his/her day-to-day leadership. Role play these scenarios to provide the leader with experience discussing differences in values.

HANDOUT 4
VALUES AND INDIVIDUAL
ACTIONS WORKSHEET

Directions: Take turns drawing one card each from your Values Card decks. Once you have each drawn three cards, assume that these values are associated with three people working together on a project or process.

ROUND 1

- Each person draws one value card. List those values here:

_____

_____

_____

_____

- As a first step, discuss with your group how each of you would define the values. You'll note that there are not only variations in what we value, but in how we define each value. Take five minutes to do this.
- Use the following questions for your discussion. Take notes in the space provided.

- What challenges might be presented if these were the three primary values of the team members.

_____

_____

_____

_____

_____

- How might they overcome these challenges?

_____

_____

_____

_____

- If you were the leader of this group (they report to you or you are responsible for the project), what might you do to facilitate communication and collaboration for this group?

  _____

  _____

  _____

  _____

- What if the values are similar? What challenges or benefits might this involve? How can the team members overcome these risks?

  _____

  _____

  _____

  _____

Be prepared to share examples with the group.

ROUND 2

- Each person draws one value. List those values here:

_____

_____

_____

_____

_____

- As a first step, discuss with your group how each of you would define the values. You'll note that there are not only variations in what we value, but in how we define each value. Take five minutes to do this.
- Use the following questions for your discussion. Take notes in the space provided.
  - What challenges might be presented if these were the three primary values of the team members.

_____

_____

_____

_____

_____

- How might they overcome these challenges?

  _____

  _____

  _____

  _____

- If you were the leader of this group (they report to you or you are responsible for the project), what might you do to facilitate communication and collaboration for this group?

  _____

  _____

  _____

  _____

- What if the values are similar? What challenges or benefits might this involve? How can the team members overcome these risks?

_____

_____

_____

_____

_____

Be prepared to share examples with the group.

ROUND 3

- Each person draws one value. List those values here:

_____

_____

_____

_____

- As a first step, discuss with your group how each of you would define the values. You'll note that there are not only variations in what we value, but in how we define each value. Take five minutes to do this.
- Use the following questions for your discussion. Take notes in the space provided.
  - What challenges might be presented if these were the three primary values of the team members.

_____

_____

_____

_____

- How might they overcome these challenges?

_____

_____

_____

_____

- If you were the leader of this group (they report to you or you are responsible for the project), what might you do to facilitate communication and collaboration for this group?

_____

_____

_____

_____

- What if the values are similar? What challenges or benefits might this involve? How can the team members overcome these risks?

_____

_____

_____

_____

_____

Be prepared to share examples with the group.

ACTIVITY 7
CASE STUDIES: VALUES AS COACHING TOOLS

ACTIVITY OVERVIEW

In this activity, leaders use case studies to challenge themselves to determine how to use values in everyday leadership situations.

PURPOSE

To challenge leaders to use values to help them address everyday leadership situations. As a result of this activity, leaders will be able to:

- Utilize the The Leadership Challenge Values Cards to help identify values that are important to address any leadership challenge.
- Determine an approach to challenging leadership situations using the TLC Values.

PARTICIPANTS

Minimum: 3
Maximum: 40
Recommended: 12 to 15
   (Participants work in groups of three during in this activity.)

PREREQUISITES

One of the earlier activities, such as "Leaders Tell Us . . . (Activity 2) and/or Values Card Sort (Activity 3).

TIME

60 minutes, which includes setup, the activity, and a debriefing

SUPPLIES AND RESOURCES

- The Leadership Challenge Values Card deck for each group
- The Leadership Challenge Values Case Studies handout (number 5)
- Our Real Work Situations and Values handout (number 6)
- The Leadership Challenge Values Card Deck for each participant to take away if not already provided

FACILITATOR NOTES

Overview

We often think of values from our own perspectives, analyzing how we align our own actions to the values that we profess. Values can also be a wonderful aid to help us collaborate with others, helping us communicate with others in a way that is more effective.

In this activity, case studies will be used to enable participants to learn how to utilize values so that they can begin to apply them to their own leadership challenges. As a result, they should be able to use values to help them address everyday leadership situations, utilizing the The Leadership Challenge Values Cards to help identify values that are important to address any leadership challenge. They will also be able to determine an approach to challenging leadership situations using the TLC Values.

Activity Setup

- Divide participants into table groups of three or four. Ask them to sit at their tables so they can play a card game, with the tables clear of materials and other workshop items.

- Distribute one deck of The Leadership Challenge Values Cards per table.
- Distribute copies of the TLC Values Case Studies to all participants.

Introduce the Activity

Have participants read Case Study 1 and have a brief table discussion about the key points noted in Questions 1 through 4 on the Case Studies handout. Have participants take notes on their handouts. Allow ten to fifteen minutes.

- *What are the values that come into play in this workplace challenge?*
- *Who is impacted as a result of the challenge, issue, or situation?*
- *How does the challenge, issue, or situation affect relationships?*
- *How does the challenge, issue, or situation affect organization/unit/team results?*

Once they have read and discussed Case Study 1, the participants will have an opportunity to share their ideas about how to handle this situation with their table group members using the values in a fun and meaningful activity.

Play the Game

For the first round, provide the following instructions one step at a time to get the groups accustomed to the process they will use for the activity. Afterward, they will cycle the rounds on their own.

- *Step 1:* Each team selects a dealer. The dealer shuffles the cards and deals them out to everyone in the table group. Deal out all the cards in the deck. Some individuals may have more cards than others. (Step 1 takes about one minute.)

- *Step 2:* Each person reviews his/her "hand." Each participant mentally selects one of the values from the The Leadership Challenge Values Cards he/she is holding that could BEST help address the situation/problem in the Case Study. (Step 2 takes three or four minutes.)

- *Step 3:* Starting with the person to the left of the dealer, each participant takes a turn by placing the selected The Leadership Challenge Values Card in the center of the table. Each player reads the value aloud and explains how this value can address the situation. Each participant should place one card in the center of the table. (Step 3 takes six to eight minutes.)

- *Step 4:* Once your group is finished, complete Question 5 from the TLC Values Case Studies handout, including an action plan using the values you identified. Often there are one or two values that are most applicable as first steps to resolving the issue. These should appear first in the action plan. (Step 4 takes five minutes)

- *Step 5:* Debrief Round 1/first case study with all table groups, using Questions 6, 7, and 8 on the TLC Values Case Studies handout.

Complete the Activity

Have the table groups start Round 2 and repeat Steps 1 through 5 with a new case study. Choose a new dealer. Afterward, continue with rounds until all the table groups have completed Steps 1 through 5 for each of the three case studies.

Debrief

Ask participants the following questions, and probe for more information when necessary:

- *How did the situations in the case studies compare to those in your own workplace?*

- *What did you learn about applying the values to specific workplace situations?*
- *What were some of the values behaviors that you were able to apply?*
- *Do you find yourself applying this in the regular course of your day now? Why or why not?*
- *How might you apply these or other values to your own workplace situations?*

Wrap Up

The focus for this activity was to learn more about how values can help leaders create an approach to case studies so that they can practice and eventually use values to help them address their own leadership challenges.

Encourage participants to be observant of their own leadership challenges, issues, and situations and to think through the list of questions on their own. They can also share the values with their work teams, peers, and managers to tackle real workplace issues as they arise, using them as avenues to solutions.

Thank the group for their participation.

- Distribute Our Real Work Situations and Values (Handout 6).
- Distribute one The Leadership Challenge Values Card deck per participant if they do not yet have their own decks.

VARIATIONS

1. **Case Study by Group:** If you are short on time, participants can be divided into three groups, each focusing on one of the case studies. Since participants will have the opportunity to review only one case, allowing each group to share its case and conclusions in the debriefing is important. Ask each group to select a spokesperson to briefly share:

91

- The scenario
- The most important value
- The action they would take with that value

2. **Three Meetings:** If short amounts of time are available over a period, participants can focus on one case study per meeting. This also allows reinforcement of the values over time as well as practice using the cards. It creates a "coaching circle" wherein leaders coach and are coached by each other.

3. **Take a Different Perspective:** Assigning one of several perspectives deepens the analysis of the case studies. (*Note:* The depth of discussion in this option may require adding time to the activity.)
   - This variation works best in groups of three.
   - For example, participants are asked to take one of the following perspectives in analyzing the issue (you may add those that are appropriate to your environment):
     - Manager
     - Peer
     - Human Resources Director
     - Direct Report
     - Customer (Internal or External)
   - From this perspective they choose the Value Cards they think most appropriate. For example, if looking from the perspective of a direct report in Case Study 1, a participant may choose "competence" rather than "teamwork" because he or she is most concerned with the quality of the product, not with working with others to achieve the deadline.
   - Debrief the activity asking those who took each perspective to report how they viewed the challenge differently. Ask:
     - How did your perspective impact the values that you chose?
     - In what kinds of situations may you want to take on these different perspectives in order to analyze an issue?

(Bonus! What behavior does this represent? "Harmony" or "Open-Mindedness.")

- If focusing on one case only, end here. If focusing on all three cases, either divide participants among three teams or have group members switch roles for each of the three cases.

4. **Role Play:** Allowing leaders to role play using the values provides a way for leaders to practice in a controlled environment. Speaking the words they would use in an actual situation challenges leaders and provides a great learning opportunity. To create a role play at the end of the case studies based on the roles demonstrated in Variation 3 above, follow the steps below.
   - Logistics:
     - To offer each participant a chance to lead a role play, use all three case studies.
     - This will add approximately thirty minutes per case study, ninety minutes overall.
     - The ideal number of participants per group is three. This allows each person to play the role of leader. If there are more than three people in a group, they can repeat one of the case studies in order to practice the behaviors.
   - Have participants select who will be the leaders in Case Studies 1, 2, and 3. As each case study begins, non-leaders will role play the other characters in the scenario. For example, in Case Study 1, there will be a leader and a participant playing the role of Ken. If there are more participants than roles, as is the case here, ask the remaining people to observe and take notes.
   - Using the notes they have taken about which values they'd use and how, the leader will address the other characters regarding the issue. Allow approximately five minutes for the leader to write a few bullet points for how he/she would approach the issue.
   - Create the following flip chart to provide direction:

1. Form groups of three people.
2. Choose Leaders:
   - Role Play 1 (Case Study 1): _____
   - Role Play 2 (Case Study 2): _____
   - Role Play 3 (Case Study 3): _____
3. Leaders all spend five minutes, bullet points on what you will say
4. Role Play 1: Who will be Jeremy, Heather? Observer?
5. Conduct the role play: ten minutes
6. Give feedback: ten minutes
7. Switch to next role play: switch leaders, characters

- Conduct the role play and allow time for feedback to the leaders about how well they used the leadership behaviors.
- Debrief by asking the following questions:
  - *What did you learn about demonstrating the value you chose?*
  - *What was difficult about the role play?*
  - *What did you see as observers or other characters that was done effectively by the leaders?*
  - *As leaders, what did you think you could have done better?*
  - *How will what you have learned help you with the situation you addressed?*
  - *How will this role-play activity impact the way that you demonstrate your values in your daily work?*

COACH'S NOTES

If you are working one-on-one with a leader, you can adapt this activity.

1. **Case Studies:** Rather than dealing all the cards out, you may choose to use only half or one-fourth of the deck, splitting the cards between you. Each of you then selects two or three values that would apply to each case study and you determine the approach to the situation together, focusing on one case study per meeting.

2. **Role Plays:** After determining an approach to the case study, discuss the steps that the leader would take to implement the action plan. Ask what the leader would do, how he/she would do it and what he/she would say, following the role-play instructions in Variation 4 above.

HANDOUT 5
TLC VALUES CASE STUDIES

CASE STUDY 1

A colleague of yours, Ken, is working on a project with you and is not holding his team members accountable for deadlines. Ken feels that the timelines are too aggressive and insists that the quality of the project is not to the level that is needed. You disagree, believing the deadlines are appropriate.

1. What are the values that come into play in this workplace challenge?

_____

_____

2. Who is impacted as a result of the challenge, issue, or situation?

_____

_____

3. How does the challenge, issue, or situation affect relationships?

_____

_____

4. How does the challenge, issue, or situation affect organization/ unit/team results?

    _____

    _____

5. Which values did you and your group select? What specific actions would you take to address this challenging situation with each value, and in what sequence? Create your action plan here:

    Value 1 _____

    Value 2 _____

    Value 3 _____

    Value 4 _____

6. Which of The Five Practices will be developed by addressing the situation this way?

    ____ Model the Way

    ____ Inspire a Shared Vision

    ____ Challenge the Process

    ____ Enable Others to Act

    ____ Encourage the Heart

7. What have you learned about how values impact your leadership?

_____

_____

_____

8. What was valuable about exploring the scenario?

_____

_____

_____

CASE STUDY 2

As you are passing by, you overhear an associate who reports to you in a heated phone discussion with a customer. While he/she does not hang up on the customer, you can tell that the conversation ended badly.

1. Who is impacted as a result of the challenge, issue, or situation?

2. How does the challenge, issue, or situation affect relationships?

3. How does the challenge, issue, or situation affect organization/unit/team results?

The Leadership Challenge Values Cards
Copyright © 2010 by James M. Kouzes and Barry Z. Posner.
Reproduced by permission of Pfeiffer, an Imprint of Wiley. www.pfeiffer.com

4. Which values did you and your group select? What specific actions would you take to address this challenging situation with each value, and in what sequence? Create your action plan here:

   Value 1   _____

   Value 2   _____

   Value 3   _____

   Value 4   _____

5. Which of The Five Practices will be developed by addressing the situation this way?
   ___ Model the Way
   ___ Inspire a Shared Vision
   ___ Challenge the Process
   ___ Enable Others to Act
   ___ Encourage the Heart

6. What have you learned about how values impact your leadership?

   _____

   _____

7. What was valuable about exploring the scenario?

   _____

   _____

CASE STUDY 3

Your group is tasked with developing an advertising campaign to develop more business in your area. You have help from an advertising professional, but you are responsible for creating a campaign that shows what you can provide to potential and current customers.

1. Who is impacted as a result of the challenge, issue, or situation?

   _____

   _____

2. How does the challenge, issue, or situation affect relationships?

   _____

   _____

3. How does the challenge, issue, or situation affect organization/ unit/team results?

   _____

   _____

   _____

4. Which values did you and your group select? What specific actions would you take to address this challenging situation with each value, and in what sequence? Create your action plan here:

Value 1 _____

Value 2 _____

Value 3 _____

Value 4 _____

5. Which of The Five Practices will be developed by addressing the situation this way?

___ Model the Way

___ Inspire a Shared Vision

___ Challenge the Process

___ Enable Others to Act

___ Encourage the Heart

6. What have you learned about how values impact your leadership?

_____

_____

7. What was valuable about exploring the scenario?

_____

_____

HANDOUT 6
OUR REAL WORK SITUATIONS AND VALUES

Directions: This is a tool you can use to determine values to address your real-life leadership challenges, issues, and situations. Use this handout as a reflection tool for yourself—and to share with your work team, peers, and manager to tackle different issues as they arise.

Briefly describe your team/unit/organization challenge, issue, and situation:

_____

_____

_____

_____

_____

_____

Ask these questions:

1. What are the values that come into play in this challenge, issue, or situation?

   _____

2. Who is impacted as a result of the challenge, issue, or situation?

   _____

3. How does the challenge, issue, or situation affect relationships?

   _____

4. How does the challenge, issue, or situation affect organization/ unit/team results?

   _____

   Create an action plan to address each challenge, issue, or situation.

1. Which four or five TLC Values would be critical to address/resolve the situation and to help you create an action plan?

Value 1   _____

Value 2   _____

Value 3   _____

Value 4   _____

Value 5   _____

2. Which of The Five Practices will be developed by addressing the situation this way?

___ Model the Way

___ Inspire a Shared Vision

___ Challenge the Process

___ Enable Others to Act

___ Encourage the Heart

3. What have you learned about applying the TLC Values?

_____

_____

_____

_____

ACTIVITY 8
YOUR CHALLENGING
SITUATION: VALUES AS
COACHING TOOLS

ACTIVITY OVERVIEW

In this activity, leaders create their own case studies to challenge themselves to determine how to use values in everyday leadership situations.

PURPOSE

To challenge leaders to use values to help them address everyday leadership situations. As a result of this activity, leaders will be able to:

- Utilize the The Leadership Challenge Values Cards to help identify values that are important to address any leadership challenge.
- Determine an approach to challenging leadership situations using the TLC Values.

PARTICIPANTS

Minimum: 3
Maximum: 40
Recommended: 12 to 15
   (Participants work in groups of three during in this activity.)

PREREQUISITES

An activity such as Leaders Tell Us . . . (Activity 2) and/or Values Card Sort (Activity 3), plus Case Studies: Values as Coaching Tools (Activity 7).

TIME

60 minutes, which includes setup, the activity, and a debriefing

SUPPLIES AND RESOURCES

- The Leadership Challenge Values Card deck for each group
- Completed Our Real Work Situations and Values (Handout 6 from Activity 7)

FACILITATOR NOTES

Overview

We often think of values from our own perspectives, analyzing how we align our own actions to the values that we profess. Values can also be a wonderful aid to help us collaborate with others, helping us communicate with others in a way that is more effective.

In this activity, leaders will create their own case studies that will provide practice in how to utilize values so that they can begin to apply them to their own leadership challenges. As a result, they should be able to apply values to help them address everyday leadership situations, utilizing the The Leadership Challenge Values Cards to help identify values that are important to address any leadership challenge. They will also be able to determine an approach to challenging leadership situations using the TLC Values.

Activity Setup

- Divide participants into table groups of three or four. Ask them to sit at their tables so they can play a card game, with the tables clear of materials and other workshop items.
- Distribute one deck of The Leadership Challenge Values Cards per table.
- Remind participants that they will need their completed Our Real Work Situations and Values (Handout 6).

Introduce the Activity

Have participants independently complete Questions 1 and 2 on Handout 6, if they have not already done so (allow six to eight minutes for reflection):

- Briefly describe the situation, including the primary challenges and who is involved.
- Explain how this situation affects results and why these results are important.

Now they will have an opportunity to share this situation with their table groups and receive some help addressing it using the TLC Values in a fun and meaningful activity. Ask:

- *What are the values that come into play in this workplace challenge?*
- *Who is impacted as a result of the challenge, issue, or situation?*
- *How does the challenge, issue, or situation affect relationships?*
- *How does the challenge, issue, or situation affect organization/unit/team results?*

Once they have discussed the first leader's situation, the participants will have an opportunity to share their ideas about how to handle this situation with their table groups using the values in a fun and meaningful activity.

Play the Game

For the first round, provide the following instructions one step at a time to get the groups accustomed to the process they will use for the activity. Afterward, they will cycle the rounds on their own.

- *Step 1:* The leader who shared a situation is the dealer. The dealer shuffles the cards and deals them out to everyone in the table group. Deal out all the cards in the deck. Some individuals may have more cards than others. (Step 1 takes about one minute.)
- *Step 2:* Each person reviews his/her "hand." Each participant mentally selects one of the values from the The Leadership Challenge Values Cards he/she is holding that could BEST help address the situation/problem in the Case Study. (Step 2 takes three or four minutes.)
- *Step 3:* Starting with the person to the left of the dealer, each participant takes a turn by placing the selected The Leadership Challenge Values Card in the center of the table. Each player reads the value aloud and explains how this value can address the situation. Each participant should place one card in the center of the table. (Step 3 takes six to eight minutes.)
- *Step 4:* Once your group is finished, complete Question 5 from the TLC Values Case Studies handout, including an action plan using the values you identified. Often there are one or two values that are most applicable as first steps to resolving the issue. These should appear first in the action plan. (Step 4 takes five minutes.)
- *Step 5:* Debrief Round 1/first case study with all table groups, using the following questions:

- *Which of The Five Leadership Practices will be developed by addressing the situation this way?*
  - *____ Model the Way*
  - *____ Inspire a Shared Vision*
  - *____ Challenge the Process*
  - *____ Enable Others to Act*
  - *____ Encourage the Heart*
- *What have you learned about applying how values impact your leadership?*
- *What was valuable about exploring the scenario?*

Complete the Activity

Have the table groups start Round 2 and repeat Steps 1 through 5 with a new leader's case study. Afterward, continue with rounds until all the table groups have completed Steps 1 through 5 for each of the leaders.

Debrief

Ask participants the following questions, and probe for more information when necessary:

- *How did your situations compare? Were they similar? Different?*
- *What did you learn about applying values to specific workplace situations?*
- *What were some of the values that you were able to apply?*
- *Do you find yourself applying these values in the regular course of your day now? Why or why not?*
- *How might you apply these or other values to your own workplace situations?*

Wrap Up

The focus for this activity was to learn more about how values can help leaders create an approach to case studies so that they can practice and eventually use values to help them address their own leadership challenges.

Encourage participants to be observant of their own leadership challenges, issues, and situations and to think through the list of questions on their own. They can also share the values with their work teams, peers, and managers to tackle real workplace issues as they arise, using them as avenues to solutions.

Thank the group for their participation.

- Distribute one The Leadership Challenge Values Card deck per participant if they do not yet have their own decks.

VARIATIONS

1. **Three Meetings:** If short amounts of time are available over a period, participants can focus on one case study per meeting. This also allows reinforcement of the values over time as well as practice using the cards. It creates a "coaching circle" wherein leaders coach and are coached by each other.

2. **Take a Different Perspective:** Assigning one of several perspectives deepens the analysis of the case studies. (*Note:* The depth of discussion in this option may require adding time to the activity.)
   - This variation works best in groups of three.
   - For example, participants are asked to take one of the following perspectives in analyzing the issue (you may add those that are appropriate to your environment):
     - Manager
     - Peer
     - Human Resources Director
     - Direct Report
     - Customer (Internal or External)

- From this perspective they choose the Values Cards they think most appropriate. For example, if looking from the perspective of a direct report in Case Study 1, a participant may choose "competence" rather than "teamwork" because he/she is most concerned with the quality of the product, not with working with others to achieve the deadline.
- Debrief the activity asking those who took each perspective to report how they viewed the challenge differently. Ask:
  - How did your perspective impact the values that you chose?
  - In what kinds of situations may you want to take on these different perspectives in order to analyze an issue? (Bonus! What behavior does this represent? "Harmony" or "Open-Mindedness.")
- If focusing on one case only, end here. If focusing on all three cases, either divide participants among three teams or have group members switch roles for each of the three cases.

3. **Role Play:** Allowing leaders to role play using the values provides a way for leaders to practice in a controlled environment. Speaking the words they would use in an actual situation challenges leaders and provides a great learning opportunity. To create a role play at the end of the case studies based on the roles demonstrated in Variation 2 above, follow the steps below.
   - Logistics:
     - To offer each participant a chance to lead a role play, use all three case studies.
     - This will add approximately thirty minutes per case study, ninety minutes overall.
     - The ideal number of participants per group is three. This allows each person to play the role of leader. If there are more than three people in a group, they can repeat one of the case studies in order to practice the behaviors.

- Have participants select who will be the leader in Case Studies 1, 2, and 3. As each case study begins, non-leaders will role play the other characters in the scenario. For example, in Case Study 1, there will be a leader and a participant playing the role of Ken. If there are more participants than roles, as is the case here, ask the remaining people to observe and take notes.
- Using the notes they have taken about which values they'd use and how, the leader will address the other characters regarding the issue. Allow approximately five minutes for the leader to write a few bullet points for how he/she would approach the issue.
- Create the following flip chart to provide direction:

> 1. Form groups of three people.
> 2. Choose Leaders:
>   - Role Play 1 (Case Study 1): _____
>   - Role Play 2 (Case Study 2): _____
>   - Role Play 3 (Case Study 3): _____
> 3. Leaders all spend five minutes, bullet points on what you will say
> 4. Role Play 1: Who will be Jeremy, Heather? Observer?
> 5. Conduct the role play: ten minutes
> 6. Give feedback: ten minutes
> 7. Switch to next role play: switch leaders, characters

- Conduct the role play and allow time for feedback to the leaders about how well they used the leadership behaviors.
- Debrief by asking the following questions:
  - *What did you learn about using values as a tool in discussions?*

114

- *What was difficult about the role play?*
- *What did you see as observers or other characters that was done effectively by the leaders?*
- *As leaders, what did you think you could have done better?*
- *How will what you have learned help you with the situation you addressed?*
- *How will this role-play activity impact the way that you demonstrate your values in your daily work?*

COACH'S NOTES

If you are working one-on-one with a leader, you can adapt this activity.

1. **Case Studies:** Rather than dealing all the cards out, you may choose to use only half or one-fourth of the deck, splitting the cards between you. Each of you then selects two or three values that would apply to each case study and you determine the approach to the situation together, focusing on one case study per meeting.

2. **Role Plays:** After determining an approach to the case study, discuss the steps that the leader would take to implement the action plan. Ask what the leader would do, how he/she would do it, and what he/she would say, following the role-play instructions in Variation 3 above.

SHARED VALUES THAT MAKE THE DIFFERENCE ACTIVITIES

ACTIVITY 9
SHARED TEAM VALUES: KEEPING PERSONAL VALUES IN MIND

ACTIVITY OVERVIEW

In this activity, team members share their personal values with the team and discuss their commonalities and differences in order to be a more effective work group.

PURPOSE

To provide the opportunity for a team to understand why members do what they do, enabling them to be more effective as they interact with others who value different things. As a result of this activity, participants will be able to:

- Share their values with their teammates in order to provide insight to others.
- Understand the values of teammates in order to understand more about their motivations.
- Utilize ground rules around how they interact based on both values that are common and those that are distinct.

PARTICIPANTS

Minimum: 3
Maximum: 20
Best: 6 to 12
  (Participants work in one large group in this activity.)

PREREQUISITES

Values Card Sort (Activity 3)

TIME

45 to 60 minutes

SUPPLIES AND RESOURCES

- Completed Defining Your Values (Handout 2 from Activity 3) for each participant
- Post-it Notes® or index cards
- Flip charts and easels (or a laptop and projector to capture and display the discussion)
- Markers

FACILITATOR NOTES

Overview

Explain that an effective team is made up of individuals who bring their own strengths and areas of development to the table. This diversity is what helps make successful teams—teams on which the sum of the parts create more than can be accomplished individually.

At times, the differences can cause conflicts, while the similarities can cause a lack of creativity. The more we are aware of our similarities and differences, the more we can focus on our success. Say to the participants:

To become aware of what is important to each of us, we are going to take the values that we created in our Values Card Sort and explore the individual values that our team holds. This will provide the opportunity for us to understand why members do what they do, enabling us to be more effective as we interact with others who value different things. During this activity, we will share our values with others on the team in order to gain insight about each other. We need to understand the values of teammates in order to understand more about their motivations and communication styles. Finally, we will create some ground rules around how we interact in the future based on values we hold in common and those that are distinct.

Activity Setup

Explain the process by saying:

- *Each of you has five Post-it Notes.*
- *At the top of each note, write your name, and in the center, write one of your top five values until you have written five notes each with one of your five values.*
- *One-by-one, we will post our values on the flip charts at the front of the room.*
- *As each person goes to the chart, he or she will share the value and his or her definition of that value.*
- *Then, as a group, we will decide what values are similar and should be grouped together, discussing these as well as any differences as we progress.*
- *This will help us better understand why we do what we do and what each of us finds important in our work.*

Encourage team members to share their definitions of their values as well as the names of the values.

Complete the Activity

Once you have the values grouped on a flip chart, make observations about the values that are similar, as well as those that are different.

Debrief

Ask the following questions to debrief (add your own ideas based on the groupings):

- *What do you think this grouping of values says about our team?*
- *What are some examples you've seen in our team lately of these common values?*
- *What challenges do you think this grouping might pose?*
- *What might be some ground rules that we want to use now that we know each other's values?*
    (Possible answers: respect each other's values; keep values in mind when conflicts arise; discuss values to build bridges with each other; etc.)

Put the responses on a flip chart and retype them to send out to the group at a later time.

Wrap Up

Share with participants:

- *Being aware of your own values, as well as those of others, can enhance the work of any team. As a team, we now have more knowledge than we've had before about why we each do what we do. This knowledge can help us in our future success.*

Thank the group for their participation.

(Note: After the activity, create a visual that each team member can keep on his/her desk as a reminder of shared values, as well as those that are different. See Figure 9.1 for a sample.)

FIGURE 9.1. Sample Illustration of Team Values

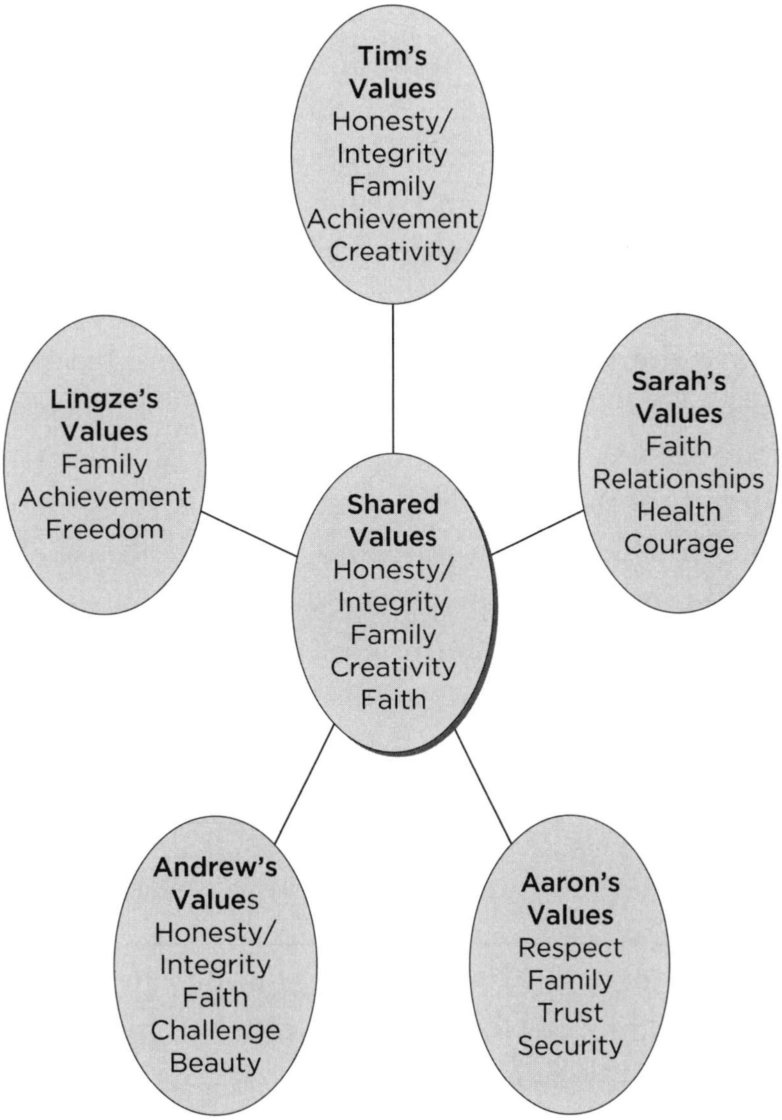

VARIATIONS

1. **Human Billboard:** If participants conducted the Human Billboard in Activity 3 (Values Card Sort), have them bring along the flip charts that they completed in that session. If not, have participants create a "human billboard" whereby they communicate their values using visual symbols. Each participant receives a page of flip-chart paper and draws one, or all, of his/her values on the page (depending on the amount of time available).

2. **Values Metaphor for Team**: After conducting the activity, create a Values Metaphor for the team. A Values Metaphor draws on metaphors, pictures, and words to give a big picture of the values of a team. Follow the instructions below to conduct this activity. Allow thirty to forty-five additional minutes for this variation.
   - Gather flip-chart paper, markers, and the chart with your Shared Team Values.
   - As a team, review the Shared Team Values and their commonalities and brainstorm metaphors for the group. For example, "Our team is like a jet. It's fast, sleek, and aimed toward our goals" for an achievement-focused group or "Our team is like Jack and the Beanstalk, with the sun representing the energy that fuels our growth and the stalks representing the support we give each other."
   - Once a metaphor has been agreed on, put two flip-chart sheets together and nominate a team member(s) to draw the metaphor. You can use words and pictures to describe the metaphor, but the picture is key to providing a symbol of your values.
   - Post in a common area, or have small copies made for each team member, to accompany the list of team values you've created (see Figure 9.1).

COACH'S NOTES

If you are working one-on-one with a leader, you can adapt this activity. You may have the leader work through the activity with his/her team first, and then discuss how the similarities and differences can be focus areas in determining how he/she best works with the team.

ACTIVITY 10
CREATING TEAM VALUES

ACTIVITY OVERVIEW

In this activity, team members build on their personal values to create team (or department, division, etc.) values.

PURPOSE

To provide the opportunity for a group to create team values based on their own personal values that can help guide them as they move toward their objectives.

PARTICIPANTS

Minimum: 3
Maximum: 40
Best: 12 to 20
   (Participants work in groups of four or five during this activity.)

PREREQUISITES

Values Card Sort (Activity 3) and Shared Team Values (Activity 9)

TIME

45 to 60 minutes

SUPPLIES AND RESOURCES

- Visual of Team's Individual and Shared Values (in handouts, poster or PowerPoint slide format; see Figure 9.1 on page 119 for a sample)
- The Leadership Challenge Values Card deck for each small group
- Index cards
- Copy of the company/organizational values for Variation 1
- Flip-chart paper and an easel
- Markers

FACILITATOR NOTES

Overview

Explain that an effective team is made up of individuals who bring their own strengths and areas of development to the table. This diversity is what helps make successful teams—where the sum of the parts create more than can be accomplished individually. When team members have discovered their own personal values, members can create team values that can apply to the entire team or department to guide them as they work toward shared goals.

Activity Setup

Say to the group:

- *Our shared values are posted here (show visual of Shared Values). They will be the starting point for our team values.*

- *You might be thinking "How can 'family' be a team value." Well, if we all determine that balancing family with our work is critical, we could make it a value and align our actions with that. If, however, we determine other values as more appropriate for our goals, we may take that one off of our team list.*

- *To determine which are our team's "top five" values, we are going to work on this activity in groups.*

Begin the Activity

Form small teams of four or five.

Step 1: Have each team brainstorm values that may be helpful for the team to achieve goals and function as an effective team.

- Team members should use the shared values, as well as the The Leadership Challenge Values Card deck, to come up with no more than ten possible values. If there is a value that is not listed on the Values Cards, the team can write this value on a blank card or an index card.

Step 2: Just as in the personal values exercise (Activity 2), each team will now determine the five values that they think will be most important for this group or part of the organization.

- Have each team member write his or her five values and a definition of what that value means to him or her on a separate index card. Each of them should have no more than five index cards.
- Each team then works together to choose the five values that represent them as a team. This process will take fifteen or twenty minutes.

Step 3: Have each group select a spokesperson to present the group's five values and bring all of the spokespeople to one location in the room.

- That group will now be tasked with determining which five of the values from all of the groups will be the set of team values for this group.
- Each spokesperson shares the values and definitions that his or her group came up with.
- The spokespeople group similar values and ultimately determine the large group's top five values.

Step 4: Once the spokespeople determine the top five values, the leader or facilitator writes the values one-by-one on a flip chart and asks the following questions about each one:

- *What is the definition of the value from the index card?*
- *Can we each buy into this value as being one of our guiding values? If not, why not? What may need to be changed?*

(Note: be prepared for some "back and forth" on definitions, or even the "title" of the value. Allow time for good discussion.)

The values the entire group comes up with can now be used as guideposts for the entire team. Each team member can manage his/her behavior by these values and can also feel comfortable in pointing out when the team has strayed away from these values.

(Note: you may want to brainstorm ideas on how the team can create reminders around these values. Examples may include creating posters or signs for the work area; putting the values at the top of all meeting agendas/requests; incorporating these values into a shared team values chart and ensuring that each team member has a copy, etc.)

Debrief

Ask the following questions to debrief (or add your own ideas based on the grouping):

- *What do you think this grouping of values says about our team?*
- *What challenges do you think living up to these values might pose?*
- *What might be some ground rules that we want to use now that we know each other's values and also have team values?*

Wrap Up

Share with participants:

- *Being aware of your own values, as well as those of others, can enhance the work of any team. As a team, we now have more knowledge than we've had before about why we each do what we do. This will help us in our future success.*

Thank the group for their participation.

VARIATIONS

1. **Company/Organizational Values:** If your company or organization has posted values, add those to the list of potential values that the team can choose. Have a copy of the values for each group to utilize, and explain that the organizational values provide the overarching values for how they accomplish their work. Ask the group to consider which, if any, of these values are particularly important for their team. If so, they can include these in the values that they choose for their small groups.

2. **Values Metaphor for Team**: If you've created a metaphor map for the shared personal values in Activity 9 that the team has, you may want to adapt it or complete a new map for the team values. The values metaphor draws on metaphors, pictures, and words to give a big picture of the values of a team. Follow the instructions below to conduct this activity. Allow thirty to forty-five minutes additional for this activity.
   - Gather flip-chart paper, markers, and the chart with your shared team values.
   - As a team, review the shared team values and commonalities, and brainstorm metaphors for the group. For example, "Our team is like a jet . . . it's fast, sleek, and aimed toward our goals" for an achievement-focused group or "Our team is like Jack and the Beanstalk, with the sun representing the energy that fuels our growth, and the stalks representing the support we give each other."
   - Once a metaphor has been agreed on, put two flip-chart sheets together and nominate a team member(s) to draw

the metaphor. They can use words and pictures to describe the metaphor, but the picture is key to providing a symbol of their values.

- Post in a common area, or have small copies made for each team member to accompany the list of team values they've created (see Figure 9.1).

3. **Create a Team Vision:** Once the group has team values in place, they may want to look into the future and discuss what the future will look like. They might consider what their team goals are currently, as well as what they want the team to achieve in the more distant future (three to six years from now). Use the following questions to create discussion, and ultimately their vision for the future.*

- *What is your ideal work community? What do you personally aspire to create?*

- *What is unique about your hopes, dreams, and aspirations? How are these distinctive compared to all other visions of the future?*

- *When you project this vision into the future ten to fifteen years, what does it look like? What innovations and trends will influence that future? What vision will carry you forward into the future?*

- *What images come to mind when thinking of the future? What does it look like, sound like, taste like, and feel like?*

- *How does this vision serve the common good? What are the shared aspirations among all the constituents? How does the vision fulfill others ideal and unique images of the future?*

These questions are reprinted with permission from Kouzes and Posner, The Leadership Challenge (4th ed.), page 153. For additional resources, review Section 3, Chapters 5 and 6, in The Leadership Challenge (4th ed.) regarding Envision the Future and Enlist Others.

COACH'S NOTES

If you are working one-on-one with a leader, you can adapt this activity. While you may discuss the activity with the leader from a planning standpoint, emphasize that he/she is part of the team. You might suggest that he/she sit in one of the small groups to complete the exercise. Coach the leader on how to help the team hold itself accountable for using the values and values map as guides for how they interact—not expecting perfection, but using the values as discussion points when things do not go as expected.

The leader may want to create his/her own vision of the future prior to this session if he/she will be creating a team vision. If so, review Section 3, Chapters 5 and 6, in *The Leadership Challenge* (4th ed.) regarding Envision the Future and Enlist Others with the leader. This provides a rich resource, with a number of reflection questions that can be utilized in coaching the leader on his/her vision.

ACTIVITY 11
ORGANIZATIONAL, TEAM, AND PERSONAL VALUES IN ACTION

ACTIVITY OVERVIEW

In this activity, participants examine the relationships between organizational values and their personal values in order to determine where they are aligned.

PURPOSE

To provide the opportunity for participants to examine the relationship between organizational and personal values. As a result of this activity, participants will be able to:

- Identify what personal values align with organizational values.
- Identify situations in which organizational values are in use and determine alternative actions to take utilizing the values when they are not evident in their own or others' actions.

PARTICIPANTS

Minimum: 3
Maximum: 40
Best: 12 to 20
    (Participants work in groups of three to five during this activity.)

PREREQUISITES

Values Card Sort (Activity 3), Shared Team Values (Activity 9), and Creating Team Values (Activity 10)

TIME

60 minutes for Part 1 and 45 minutes for Part 2

SUPPLIES AND RESOURCES

- The Leadership Challenge Values Card deck for each small group
- Completed copy of Defining Your Values (Handout 2 from Activity 3)
- Copy of the Company/Organizational Values (see Variation 1 if these do not exist)
- Visual of Team's Individual and Shared Values (in handout, poster, or PowerPoint slide format; see Figure 9.1 on page 119 for a sample)
- Organizational Values in Action handout (number 7).
- Flip chart and easel
- Markers

FACILITATOR NOTES

Overview

Explain in your own words that, as Kouzes and Posner say, "Values . . . serve as guides to action. They inform our decisions as to what to do and what not to do; they tell us when to say yes, or no, and help us really understand why we mean it" (*The Leadership Challenge*, 4th ed., pp. 52–53.

Say that this includes our personal values, as well as organizational values. As research by Kouzes and Posner has shown, our personal values drive our commitment to an organization (*The Leadership Challenge*, 4th ed., pp. 54–57). Knowing our own values has a large influence on how committed we are to our organizations. On the other hand, having shared organizational values that serve as guides to actions also has a great impact on success. Research shows that organizations with strong cultures based on values have much greater revenue growth, job creation, increase in their stock prices and profit performance (*The Leadership Challenge*, 4th ed., p. 63).

Say: *"Today, we'll have the opportunity to examine the relationships between organizational and personal values. As a result of this activity, you will be able to identify which of your personal values align with organizational values, identify situations in which organizational values are in use, and determine alternative actions to take utilizing the values when these are not evident in others' actions."*

Activity Setup
- Divide participants into table groups of three or four. Ask them to clear the table of materials and other workshop items so that they can utilize the The Leadership Challenge Values Cards.
- Distribute one deck of The Leadership Challenge Values Cards per table.
- Distribute a copy of the organization's values (if they exist) to each participant.
- Have a flip-chart stand or pages available to each small group.

Begin the Activity
Part I: How do organizational values and personal values intersect?

- Step 1: Have each group address one of the organizational values.
  - For example, if the organizational values are Trustworthy, Personal, Empathetic, Collaborative, and Proactivity, you will have five groups, one per value.
- Step 2: Each team will now match the TLC Values to the organizational values.
  - Have one person in each group deal out all of the The Leadership Challenge Values Cards to other members of his/her group.
  - Tell them to, one-by-one, go through the cards in their hands and put in the middle of the table those that match with the organizational value they have been assigned. It may be that the values selected **define** the organizational value or that it is a value that is **similar** to the organizational value. Emphasize that there are no right answers, and that this process is simply to create discussion.
  - For example, if they are looking at "Proactivity," they might pull out the values Innovation, Productivity, Risk Taking, Autonomy, and Independence.
  - Each group is to select one or two values per person and write the organizational value at the top of a flip-chart sheet with the TLC Values listed below it. Allow fifteen minutes.
- Step 3: Once each group has completed a flip chart, have them review their own Personal Values and the Shared Team Values from their completed Defining Your Values handouts (number 2) and Shared Team Values visual (as illustrated in the sample in Figure 9.1 on page 119).
  - First have each group look at the organization's values in terms of their own personal values. Have them mark a "P"

next to any of the listed organizational values that coincide with their personal values.

- Next have each group look at the organization's values in terms of their team values, and mark a "T" next to each of the listed organizational values that coincides with their team values.

- Step 4: Debrief by having each team choose a spokesperson. Have the spokespeople share with the large group the organizational value, the TLC Values, and where these overlap with personal and shared team values. Allow fifteen to twenty-five minutes for presentations and then ask the following questions:

- *In what way are organizational values defined by, or common to, the TLC Values?*

- *Were there any organizational values that were difficult to compare to the TLC Values? Why do you think this is? What does that mean for us as we use the organizational values as guides?*

- *In what way are the organizational values similar to your own values?*

- *Were there any organizational values that were difficult to compare to your own values? Why do you think this is?* (Emphasize that this doesn't necessarily mean that their values are not aligned with the organization's and that just because a value is different does not mean that it is bad to have.)

- *In what way are the organizational values similar to your shared team values?*

- *Were there any organizational values that were difficult to compare to the team values? Why do you think this is?* (Emphasize that this doesn't necessarily mean that their values are not aligned with the organization and that just because a value is different does not mean it is bad to have.)

Say: *"The organizational values will now be our focus. We'll look at how we can use them as guides to our behavior on a daily basis in our work."*

Part 2: How do we see organizational values in action?

(Note: You may want to have participants change their groups in order to benefit from different perspectives.)

- *Step 1:* Have each participant complete the Organizational Values in Action handout. Allow them to pick the value(s) they have seen examples of recently. The examples can be based on what they've seen of others or examples when they used or did not use the values. Each participant will write:
  - One **positive** example of when a specific organizational value was evident in an interaction, project, etc., and what the outcome was.
  - One example of when a specific organizational value **could have or should have** been utilized in an interaction, project, etc. What was the outcome, and what would have changed if they had utilized that value?
- *Step 2:* Have participants pair up and share their examples. Instruct them to be aware of confidentiality if the situations are sensitive.

Debrief

Ask the following questions of participants:

- *What were some examples of when organizational values were utilized to positively guide your own or others' actions? What were the outcomes?*

- *What were some examples of when organizational values were not utilized in a situation? What were the outcomes? What suggestions did you have to change the situation? What might the new outcomes be?*
- *What observations can you make about organizational values?*
- *How might we, as a team, use these to guide how we interact? How do we apply this insight to our own team values?*

Wrap Up

Say the following in order to wrap up the activity:

- *Using organizational values as guides to our behavior can enhance the way we work together. Today, we examined the relationship between organizational and personal values. As a result, we should be able to identify what personal values align with organizational values and identify situations when organizational values are in use and determine alternative actions to take utilizing the values when they are not evident in our own or others' actions.*

Thank the group for their participation.

VARIATIONS AND ADDITIONAL ACTIVITIES

1. **What Values Do You See in Your Organization?** If your company or organization does not have posted values, ask the group to consider what values they see in how the organization goes about its work. Are Innovation, Risk Taking, and Creativity

rewarded, or are Quality, Dependability, and Service important? Have the group do a quick The Leadership Challenge Values Card sort focused on the organization and list the resulting values on a flip chart. (See Activity 3 for a general process.)

2. **Intact Team vs. Dispersed Group:** If the group is intact, ensure that they have all of the documents they need. If the group is a dispersed group of participants, ensure that they bring their own personal and team values to the session.

3. **Without Activity 9 or Activity 10:** If you have not completed the Shared Team Values or Creating Team Values activities, you can still use Activity 11 by simply adjusting the language in the instructions.

4. **Role Play Values Interactions:** Allowing leaders to role play using organizational values provides a way for leaders to practice in a controlled environment. Speaking the words they would use in an actual situation challenges leaders and provides a great learning opportunity. To create a role play at the end of Part 2 above, follow the steps below.
   - Logistics:
     - The ideal number of participants per group is three. This allows each person to play the role of leader.
     - This will add approximately thirty minutes per leader or ninety minutes overall.
   - Have participants select who will go first, second, and third in leading their own role plays. As each role play begins, non-leaders will play the other characters in the scenario based on the instruction by the leader.
   - For example, if the leader is role playing how to use the organizational value of "Empathy" there would be the leader and two participants playing roles chosen by the leader (perhaps two direct reports or a colleague and an observer). If there are more participants than roles, ask the remaining people to observe and take notes.

- For example, in Role Play 1, there will be a leader and participants playing two roles chosen by the leader (perhaps two direct reports or a colleague and an observer). If there are more participants than roles, ask the remaining people to observe and take notes.
- Using the notes they have taken on the organizational Values in Action Worksheet (number 3), the leader will role play a situation in which the organizational value was not utilized and address the other characters regarding the issue.
  Allow approximately five minutes for the leaders to write a few bullet points for how they would approach the issue.
- Create the following flip chart to provide direction:

---

1. Get into groups of three people.
2. Choose leaders:
   - Role Play 1 (Leader 1): _____
   - Role Play 2 (Leader 2): _____
   - Role Play 3 (Leader 3): _____
3. Leaders all spend five minutes; list bullet points on what you will say.
4. Role Play 1: What are the roles and who will play them? Observer?
5. Conduct the role play: ten minutes.
6. Give feedback: ten minutes.
7. Switch to next role play: switch leaders, characters

- Conduct the role play and allow time for feedback to the leaders about how well they used the alternative action taken based on the organizational value.

- Debrief by asking the following questions:
  - *What did you learn about taking actions based on organizational values?*
  - *What was difficult about the role play?*
  - *What did you see as observers or other characters that was done effectively by the leaders?*
  - *As leaders, what did you think you could have done better?*
  - *How will what you have learned help you with the situation you addressed?*
  - *How will this role-play activity impact the way that you demonstrate your values in your daily work?*

COACH'S NOTES

If you are working one-on-one with a leader, you can adapt this activity. When utilizing the activity notes from Part 1 above, pay particular attention to how the leader's personal values align with the organizational values. Discuss where there are disconnects and what impact this has on his/her leadership of others. Part 2 offers a rich dialogue using the questions included regarding organizational values as guides to the leader's own as well as others' behaviors. Add your own questions based on your experience with the leader, encouraging him/her to think about how he/she can use organizational values to build consensus and to recognize those who demonstrate the values.

HANDOUT 7
ORGANIZATIONAL
VALUES IN ACTION

*"Values . . . serve as guides to action.
They inform our decisions as to what to
do and what not to do; they tell us when
to say yes, or no, and help us really
understand why we mean it."*
—*Jim Kouzes and Barry Posner*

Think of one ***positive*** example of when a specific organizational value was evident in an interaction, project, etc.

What was the value? _____

What was the outcome?

_____

_____

_____

The Leadership Challenge Values Cards
Copyright © 2010 by James M. Kouzes and Barry Z. Posner.
Reproduced by permission of Pfeiffer, an Imprint of Wiley. www.pfeiffer.com

Now think of an example of when a specific organizational value *could have* or ***should have*** been utilized in an interaction, project, etc.

What was the value? _____

What was the outcome?

_____

_____

_____

_____

_____

_____

_____

What could have been done differently to utilize the organizational value?

_____

_____

_____

_____

_____

_____

_____

What would have changed in the outcome if this organizational value had been utilized?

_____

_____

_____

_____

_____

_____

_____